To my wife, who has been my support the entire time and for her patience,

My son, for his existence,

My mother for her pains,

And my siblings

Special thanks to my wife, my son, and my daughter-in-law for helping me with editing and encouraging me to publish this book.

MOHAMMAD SHIDFAR

The war wasn't a blessing!

CONTENTS

Iran 1

Jordan 32

Bahrain 49

Canada 82

Glossary 98

Prologue

Shah: *Cyrus! Sleep peacefully for we are awake!*

Khomeini: *The issue of Karbala, which itself is at the forefront of political issues, must remain alive!*

One called himself the king of kings, the other the leader of the world's Muslims.
Both pursued the same goal, in different ways, and the cost of their rivalry is one we must bear.

Both had a backward-looking perspective; our problem is neither Imam Hussein and the uprising of Karbala, nor Cyrus and the throne of Persepolis. Both are historical events and figures. The modern or postmodern world cannot be managed with such a perspective.

To be the king of kings or the leader of the world's Muslims, you must wage war!
War, this word is laden with disaster, it's not a blessing, nor is it honorable, it's a crime and a sin.

We need a better understanding of the world and the future, along with a renewed understanding of religion, while also striving to maintain separation between the state and the church.

Today's world is in dire need of peace, in all its forms: individual, familial, societal, and global. The rituals and literature of the world have changed, and only those stuck in the past cannot understand this. Only through separating religion from politics, pursuing justice, and respecting human values can we achieve relative tranquility in this world.

It should never be forgotten that war is not a blessing!

1

Iran

The war wasn't a blessing at all!
This is a brief story of my life, from childhood to adulthood, as a person who witnessed the 1979 revolution and the Iran-Iraq war, post-war experiences, and the story of my immigration as someone who survived psychological trauma due to the war. It's in contradiction to the former leader of Iran famously said that 'war is a blessing.'

During one of those hot summer days in Tehran at the early onset of the Iran-Iraq war, my father was on a mission at the frontline. We had no clue about his well-being, and we didn't even have a landline phone through which he could have contacted us to let us know how he was doing or to find out about us.

Several months had passed since he left, and we had just moved to a new place in the south of Tehran, an area that felt frightening, surrounded by strangers and people who had seized control after the 1979 revolution in Iran. Despite serving the country in the armed forces during the time of the Shah, my father continued his service and was among those soldiers deployed in the early months of the war. Before the revolution, he was on the waiting list for housing, but during the upheaval, Ruhollah Khomeini ordered people to occupy every available housing facility, including the Olympic village buildings designated for sports teams in Tehran's sports complex. Consequently, we lived in rental housing from the beginning, and when it was my father's turn, his long-awaited apartment had been occupied by someone else!

On the other hand, he obtained a plot of land in west Tehran and started building a house there. However, he couldn't afford the rent, leading to a chaotic situation. His mind was preoccupied with the war, which had commenced immediately after the revolution. Just before departing for the front line, he visited the housing authorities, inquiring about the apartment he had waited for years. They provided him with the address, but it had been taken over by an individual during the revolution.

They suggested he go and reclaim it by force if he could.

This marked the beginning of the end of our old, peaceful days. The occupant happened to be a drug trafficker who had been arrested and was awaiting the court's order due to the large volume of drugs and opioids in his possession! Regardless, my father was determined to reclaim that apartment, seeing it as the only viable solution.

He pursued legal avenues, visiting the police station and court to obtain an eviction order. Eventually, we moved to that place, a period I wished had never happened. It was a nightmare to live in that area of Tehran! But where and why was that?

It was part of Kiyan Shahr, specifically the section known as Azadi Alley, which ironically means 'Freedom Alley.' In reality, it was devoid of everything—law, humanity, culture, and more.

My father had initially planned for us to stay there temporarily until our house was built, but that plan never materialized, and we ended up spending 22 years of our lives in that place.

Even now, when I shut my eyes, the picture of the area is still in my head: the nasty smell of the open sewage canal that passed close to the building, the sheds on the other side of that sewage canal, the spiderweb-style electrical cables that illegally infiltrated the sheds and buildings, broken windows, damaged walls of corridors, bulbs, garbages, and worst of all, the gangsters.

I don't know what he thought, but if I were him, I would never do this to my family and move to this nasty place, even for a very short period.

But we were there; our unit was on the fourth floor. Most of the time, we didn't have electricity or water due to the illegal sources of electricity and water, as the builder didn't get the chance to finish the project due to the revolution, leaving it half-finished.
I was around 9, my brother was 3, and my sister had just been born. Since we moved to this area, my mom was young, around 26 years old, and my father was around 36 years old.

Imagine, with this much struggle, he left us and headed to the frontline! On that hot summer day, after an afternoon nap, we heard someone knocking on our unit door, which was strange because since we moved here, nobody had come to visit us.

Anyway, I opened the door, which I wished had never been opened! It was my middle uncle and his wife, my dad's middle brother. We hadn't seen them for a while, and it was quite weird to see them at this time of day and week.

After they entered and exchanged greetings according to Iranian culture, starting with a glass of icy saffron sherbet, my uncle asked, 'Have you heard from Akbar recently?' My dad's name was Ali Akbar, but everyone called him Akbar. You know when you have someone on the war frontline, this kind of question carries bad news for the family members!
Mom said, 'No! Have you?' And this was the beginning of the sad story! He replied, 'Yes, we heard that he got a minor injury, and they transferred him to one of the hospitals in Tabriz. Tabriz is one of the big cities in the northwest of Iran, near the Turkish border.

He said, 'I've come here to take you guys to grandma's house because they will bring him to Tehran by the weekend, and we can go to the hospital and visit him.' I looked into my mom's eyes, and tears were slowly dripping down, but she tried to control herself because of us. My sister was 3 months old at that time, and she was mostly worried about me and my brother.

So we packed some stuff and left the apartment with heavy hearts, worried about every possible thing that could happen to my father and our family. It was a hell of a time, stepping into an ambiguous future that impacted all of us.
We got into my uncle's old Citroen 2CV and took a long time to

reach the west side of the city. As I remember, it was never easy to drive around Tehran due to heavy traffic.

Finally, we arrived at grandma's home; she was living with my older uncle in the same house. That day, my older uncle wasn't home because he went to Tabriz to visit my father and stayed with him until flying back to Tehran with my father.

So, I heard that they would transfer my father to Tehran by Thursday night and supposed to admit him to the Police Hospital on Bahar Street in Tehran. The hospital was quite far from grandma's house; in a city like Tehran, no place is really close to where you are living.

After hearing that news, we decided to go to the hospital the next day. It was early Friday morning when we left and headed to the hospital.

This hospital was an old building with long corridors, mostly used by visitors as waiting rooms.

As we all waited in the corridor of the ward where my father was admitted, one by one, they went to visit. They didn't allow children into the wards, but in the end, after speaking with the security guard, I got permission to enter. I stepped in with my mother; you know, when you are 9 years old, you have no clue what is going on. Finally, we entered the room. It was a painful experience and moment, seeing your loved one laying down on a hospital bed and suffering. When I entered the room, he started vomiting blood, coughing, and moaning loudly. Suddenly, he saw me, and we made eye contact. Those eyes were full of sadness and regret because he knew he wasn't going to survive this time. He breathed with difficulty and could hardly speak. When he saw me, he said, 'I will get better soon, but in the meantime, you are the man of the house now. Take care of yourself, mom, and the children.' I didn't know what to say, just said, 'Sure!'

As I heard later, he passed away while he was admitted to the Tabriz hospital. The medical team tried their best to bring him back, and he is in Tehran now! Maybe God gave him the last chance to say goodbye to his family, or deep down, he didn't want to go because he had a lot of unfinished work: a 3-month-old daughter, a 3-year-old son, a 9-year-old son, his young wife, and an under-construction house.

I guess when a man falls down and lays on a hospital bed with severe injuries, all kinds of thoughts cross his mind. On the other hand, he knew the situation of the country and his family, I mean his mom and brothers and sisters, who had their own problems even before he got married to my mom. He came from a family that had a lot of struggles. Their father left them, and my dad took care of the entire family: 7 brothers and sisters, plus his mom. He supported them economically and emotionally until 6 of them got married, and only the last brother was living with his mom, who just joined the army for obligatory military service.
A big family like that, without government support, surely had many issues: economic, psychosocial, emotional, cultural barriers, and immaturity. But they seemed like normal people, not drug addicts and the like.

On the other hand, he knew his crazy, selfish father who left them behind in childhood. He was challenging his life and those situations now. He got three shots with a Dragunov sniper rifle, a heavy Soviet gun. One on his arm, one on his neck, and one on his back. Imagine a man connected to a tracheostomy pipe, and due to difficulties with transportation in the frontline, they had to crawl him for a long distance, causing his chest skin to peel off and leading to quadriplegia. He couldn't even move his hand!"
We went to visit him for almost a week, and then they decided to transfer him for surgery to another hospital because he needed to stay in ICU after the surgery, and this hospital had no available beds.
On the day of the transfer, I was waiting outside the building alone. When they took him out on a hospital bed, there was a brief moment when I stayed beside him. That was the last time I ever heard his voice. The only words he said to me were: 'If I get better, I won't go again and I will stay with you.' I don't know what happened to him, but these were the last words of a man who was proud to defend the country and live his entire life with honor and dignity. At the time, I didn't know what he saw or found out, but he told me, 'I'll never leave you alone!' Still, when I shut my eyes, I can hear his voice and see that exact picture. I remember that spot in the police hospital vividly.
Finally, they put him in the ambulance, and the siren sounded loudly as the ambulance left.
They transferred him to Mostafa Khomeini Hospital, which was a better-equipped hospital at the time. They took him to the surgery

room, and they performed a few surgeries to remove the bullet from his spinal column. However, after those surgeries, he lost his voice, and we never heard it again. He communicated without a voice, and we tried lip-reading. We partly understood what he tried to say, but he didn't talk much.
The next time I had the chance to visit him, he looked different. They had shaved off his beard, his voice was gone, and his body was cold. The only movement he could make was turning his head to the side of the bed.

We continued to visit him in this hospital for almost a month, taking a few buses to get there. Outside the hospital in the afternoon was crowded, with people coming from all over the country to visit their loved ones injured in the war. Some people ran businesses there, selling flowers, canned fruits, sweets, and chocolate. I think those who run such businesses and take advantage of the opportunity are always the winners.
We left Grandma's home at noon and arrived at the hospital in the afternoon during visiting hours. We carried a small carpet to sit on the sidewalk outside the hospital. If we were lucky, we could find a place near the shade of trees.

So, we became more familiar with the area, and sometimes I went inside the hospital to enjoy playing with the elevator, taking journeys through the different floors and corridors. I saw a lot of injured people arriving at the hospital on beds through the emergency entrance. I also witnessed patients coming out of surgery rooms with amputated legs, arms, and some with their intestines packed in plastic bags due to abdominal injuries.

Days passed, and we continued to visit the hospital every day. Once, while traveling on the bus during a hot summer day in Tehran, the bus driver suddenly hit the brakes. My three-year-old brother, sitting beside me, fell down and got wounded on his chin, bleeding profusely. That incident led to a relative suggesting that children shouldn't be taken to the hospital, prompting the need for someone to stay home and care for them. Eventually, someone came up with an alternative plan.
On Thursday, September 16, 1982, we were preparing to go to the hospital when my middle uncle arrived at the doorstep and conveyed the heartbreaking news. He said, 'We are not going to the hospital today. Akbar's vital signs are unstable.

The medical team tried, but they couldn't save him. He passed away today.' My mother fainted at the news, and that marked the onset of mourning and wailing. At only nine years old, I felt lost and unsure of what to do. I heard my mom saying, 'Akbar is gone, and my children are orphaned now,' as she cried inconsolably.

Everyone was searching for black clothing, customary in Iranian culture when someone passes away. Close relatives wear black for forty days as a sign of mourning. This loss was a tremendous shock for us, a psychological trauma that lingered for a long time, especially for my mother.
We had to wait until Saturday for the official funeral. On that morning, we left for the police college in Tehran. After bringing my dad's body from the college down to the nearby street, they placed his coffin, wrapped in flags, onto an ambulance.

We followed the ambulance in a bus on the long journey to Beheshte Zahra, Tehran's largest cemetery situated in the south. The first stop was the mortuary, where the deceased are washed and prepared for burial.
At the mortuary, amidst the emotional crowd awaiting their loved ones, I got lost, surrounded by the solemnity of the dead. It took me a while to find a relative and reach my dad's grave. Unfortunately, it was too late; they had already buried him. I never got the chance to say my final goodbye. My brother, saw him, but for me, it was an opportunity lost forever.
The stress took a toll on me, resulting in skin issues. Doctors prescribed numerous antibiotics, B complex and B12 vitamins, and even suggested a blood transfusion. Eventually, we turned to traditional medicine, which acted as a sedative and offered some relief. However, during that time, none of the doctors inquired about my life's history or symptoms. Their focus remained solely on treating the skin wounds, leading to delayed and prolonged treatments.

My mother's condition worsened due to the shock. She developed Lichen planus, and the excessive Corticosteroids prescribed caused additional health issues like osteoporosis. Even after 41 years, she continues to battle the consequences.
Following the funeral, customary events such as the funeral night party, third-day, fifth-day, seventh-day, forty-day, and anniversary parties, which are costly, ensued.

These events impose a financial burden on the host.
In situations where a woman loses her husband and lacks support, especially financially and emotionally from her family, problems arise. The husband's family often behaves like adversaries. Moreover, if the woman is considered attractive, her situation becomes even more challenging.
I believe the modern world isn't just about skyscrapers, airplanes, or cars; it's about communication, behavior, and interactions among people. Unfortunately, in societies governed by religious lenses and beliefs, humanity has been negatively impacted by rigid, old-school mentalities. These outdated beliefs, unable to adapt to modern times, have proven detrimental to current generations.

The downside of religion is that it doesn't seem applicable to modern times; it originated from an era when the human cortex wasn't in predominant use, relying more on the amygdala instead.
It's puzzling to consider people from thousands of years ago, who, despite being kind, engaged in conflicts, perhaps even severing limbs. How can such people be relevant models for contemporary life? These behaviors not only lack efficacy but also pose great harm to our current generation.
The hardest part of writing this book is to revisit those days I don't like to think about and write about every specific thing. It is really difficult and painful. It took years of hard work for me to rid myself of those feelings, and I really don't want to delve into the details.

I remember at the forty-day ceremony after we buried Dad, his deranged father showed up. He was a lunatic who had abandoned his family, and now he appeared out of nowhere! The question is, why is he here today?
He is aware of the country's unjust custody laws regarding children. He knows he could claim custody when his son passed away, and he might seize control of Dad's salary and the house under construction! That's why he showed up! He attempted to approach us in front of the people who came for the ceremony at Tehran cemetery, by Dad's grave. When he tried to take my little sister, my mom skillfully punched him and didn't allow him to take her; she knows him very well!

This is the last person who should have been added to our lives. After this ceremony, it seemed the party was over, and Mom needed an ironic boot to start the fight for custody of the children. When searching for the meaning of "blessing" in a dictionary, like Collins Cobuild, a blessing is something good that you are grateful for. But in religion, a blessing is not about acquiring good things or experiencing happiness. It is about aligning oneself with the Great Liberator Jesus Christ or other messengers, and you might suffer as they did hundreds of years ago.

From my experience, when a priest or Mullah uses the word 'blessing,' it means your life will be completely disrupted without a doubt. This was a fact that no one cared about when he said that the war is a blessing, not even highly educated people who graduated from famous Western universities.

Sometimes, I ask myself what they were taught in those prestigious universities like Sorbonne University. A person like Abolhassan Banisadr, elected as the first president of Iran after the 1979 revolution, tried to synthesize economy and banking from Islam!
To me, the main goals of higher education are knowledge, skill, and attitude. Changing attitude is the most important outcome. So, when someone graduates with a Ph.D. from a university and there is no change in their attitude, that university degree holds no value and is just a worthless piece of paper. Synthesize economy and banking from Islam and their holy book in the 20 and 21st century!

This person is definitely mentally challenged and should be admitted to a hospital for treatment to prevent harm to others.
So, Mom was struggling to obtain custody, and it took a few long months to achieve that, a significant challenge at the time. She fought fiercely for it. Imagine, all the laws were against her, and an uncontrollable father-in-law made it even harder.

Days passed, she left home early in the morning and returned late in the evening. On the other hand, we had a lot of debts but no income, and Dad's meager salary was cut due to this situation.

In a third world country in the midst of crisis and war, with a husband's family acting as enemies and her own family being unsupportive, three children and their responsibilities in a chaotic city like Tehran, alongside a foolish system still dealing with its issues after the Islamic revolution...

After the 40 day ceremony, we took off the black dress, but the whole perspective of life appeared darker, lacking horizons at the end! I recall that for years after, visiting my dad's grave in the cemetery became one of our favorite things . It became part of our routine - every weekend, any occasion, and holiday.

During the war, the cemetery saw a peak in visitors and funeral ceremonies, especially on weekends and Thursday evenings, which Muslims believe are important days to visit the dead. The best days of our lives seemed to be spent in the cemetery. Each visit brought more grief and sadness from others, adding to our depression and pain, causing a sense of being fed up and giving up on the world. Happiness and joy were strangers and considered sinful.

Days passed, and this continued for years - praying for the happiness of the souls of the departed and seeking forgiveness for our sins. It seemed like a significant deal. What could be better than this for the Mullahs , who have been in power since the revolution?

They engaged in a lot of propaganda, depicting martyrs as holy individuals receiving the best afterlife rewards. They crafted stories where, after getting injured and falling as angels, they'd be carried to paradise. This narrative became like a game for them, a win-win situation. People dying meant ceremonies, services by mullahs (who charged handsomely), and obtaining government positions post-revolution.

Concerts, music, and sources of happiness were banned after the revolution, and the war helped sell fear and tears for absolution and forgiveness from God. It appeared a profitable bargain for them - an easy business where mere words and stories traded on ancient beliefs.

This situation subjected our family to external and internal pressures. Internally, we suffered from grief, loneliness, and lack of support, especially for the youngest brother in our family, who would wake up at midnight crying and looking for our father. because the three years old Boy, saw how they buried his father. And everyone of us has the similar story. Completely accomplished nightmare.Externally, as family members of a martyr, we were pressured to behave a certain way, setting an example for others.

It felt like we didn't have the right to be happy. They wanted to keep us sad, molding us into role models, injecting their ideas into our minds, altering our perception of life.

This path seemed to lead only to death. The mullahs played a masterful game, showing how worthless this life is and how beautiful the afterlife could be, but they know "the shortest route to wealth is the contempt of wealth". They seemed to hold exclusive knowledge about it, encouraging people to move there while neglecting their real lives and existence in this world. Finding myself took years. I recall deciding to join the war during intermediate school. My teacher, slapped me and vehemently advised against it, stating one dead from my family was enough.

He urged me to focus on education, foreseeing an end to the war one day. He helped me catch up on missed schooling, even providing private lessons at home. Yet, ignorant neighbors still questioned his visits due to their prejudiced mindset about a teacher helping a widow's child.

Such sick mentalities and attitudes were what we encountered daily. And every day, I pondered: Where was the blessing in the war?

The lifestyle in our area is deteriorating every day, making it less desirable for those who wish not to be there.

The number of sheds increased daily, and homeless people were more likely to migrate to this area of Tehran from other parts of the country.

Unfortunately, the number of gangs and criminals increased daily in the only area of Tehran without police stations, transforming it into a lawless city.

Spiderweb-like electric cables sprawl everywhere, streetlights are broken, sewage canals have widened to resemble rivers, and homeless people have constructed shelters using waste materials like plastic and metal containers filled with sand and soil.

I recall a movie being filmed in our area from national television about Palestine and they came to our area for recording and depicting the dire conditions, particularly the foul smell from the sewage river that worsened during hot summers without electricity for coolers. Opening the windows for fresh air was impossible.

Once, I remember the Shah's son expressing disbelief on TV about the 1979 revolution and the people's monstrosity. He questioned the reason behind it.

This leads to my question for you and your father: What did you do to this country? These people are not foreigners or aliens; they've been deprived of education, economic resources, civilization, and many couldn't even speak Farsi which is the national language, it proves that they didn't even attend school.

Over more than half a century of governing the country, your family has enjoyed wealth, prestige, a luxurious life, but failed to develop and advance the nation as any other civilized country would.
I don't blame these deprived people; instead, I'm astonished that there are still individuals who live in primitive conditions.

I observed a two-bedroom unit in our building occupied by three different families, highlighting the immense hardships brought about by poverty. Nothing explains this situation better than the impact of poverty on survival.

I witnessed the bleakest aspects of life and culture in Iran's capital city, Tehran, which were both disgusting and unbelievable. I imagined all these events happening simultaneously - men fighting on the front lines for the sake of their country while people struggled daily due to poverty and a lack of educational opportunities to survive. It was a stark contrast. I observed how a lack of knowledge and understanding could lead to the worst and most dangerous consequences in a person.
Days have passed, and our situation is worsening. Despite Mom's efforts to restart construction, it's challenging. My dad's family eyes the property, claiming their share under Islamic law. Dad's will, though detailed, lacks legal registration, causing acceptance issues.

The contractor, taking advantage of chaos during revolution and war, stole construction materials, leading to a collapsed roof. In this turmoil, seeking justice against the contractor wasn't a priority, given the chaotic state of the country.
The year later, my dad's colleagues gathered together and donated the money. As volunteers, they went to the construction site to build the house and complete the construction. However, when they started working, my dad's middle brother went to the construction site and stopped them, claiming it was our house and not to allow any strangers. Later, my dad's close friend informed us about the situation, expressing sadness over the interference, which prevented them from finishing the job. This was the most significant and dreadful impact from a relative who was supposed to help us but, unfortunately, turned out to be worse than an enemy. A few years later, when I heard my uncle (my dad's middle brother) had passed away, I attended his funeral just to see his dead body and how they buried the man who caused a lot of pain and suffering for me. Everyone was aware of the reason for my presence that day.

Since then, my dad's side completely abandoned us. This happened because my mom refused to kneel in front of them, preserving her dignity. My dad's mother blamed my mom for sending him to the war, creating a foolish story in her mind that held my mom responsible for his death. She wanted custody of the children, suggesting my mom leave them and the unfinished house under construction. The reason being, my mom should let them raise the children while she could remarry. Unsure if this behavior stems from cultural poverty or religious beliefs, our house, under construction for about six years, faced challenges. After my father's death, everyone in the area finished building their houses, leaving ours unfinished. The roof collapsed once, causing a mess, and we left the construction site for a few years. Now, it resembles a garbage site, attracting homeless individuals who make fires in winter. Neighbors complained, deeming it unsafe for the community.We decided to start anew. At that time, I had a bicycle, and the distance from our current residence to our unfinished home was around 30 km.

Determined, I commuted there every day in that summer, covering a round-trip of 60 km, to clean up the mess. I brought my brother, some food, and pedaled to the construction site, working from early morning till evening—a challenging task.

Attempting to resolve matters, we contacted my dad's family, offering them their share if they'd sign the necessary papers at a lawyer's office, allowing us to finish building our house. Despite their verbal agreement, they never showed up for several appointments at the lawyer's office, rendering my hard work at the construction site futile. Additionally, over the years, inflation occurred, and the cost of materials increased, prompting our decision to sell the house.

Right after we sold the house, the cease-fire known as 598 between Iran and Iraq was accepted, causing an economic shock to the market. Everything changed rapidly; the price we received for the house couldn't even buy us an apartment in Tehran anymore. The shift was so sudden. Years later with that money, we ended up buying a washing machine, a German brand named Bosch.

All our dreams of owning a house were shattered, leaving us with only suffering, sadness, memories, and the reality of living in a place we didn't want to be. Despite our efforts, things just didn't work out for us. Sometimes, I reflect on those moments, wondering what or who I should blame.

Jealousy, revenge, religion, lack of knowledge, poor culture, and more – the only thing I understand is inflation and how any kind of change, from social to economic, happens so fast, putting our lives in a vicious cycle. Regardless of what you do or want, progress seems unattainable.

During those days, the war worsened, reaching a new phase – the cities' war. Caught between two figures, one seemingly crazier than the other, Saddam and Khomeini, life became even more challenging.

In February 1988, Saddam seemed to attack Tehran with missiles. Over 50 days, Iraq launched 189 missiles, 135 of them hitting Tehran. More than 2000 civilians lost their lives, and a quarter of Tehran's population fled. It was a terrifying time where every day, you didn't know when your time would come.
I remember the first time the missile was launched; even the Iranian forces were unsure, mistaking it for a fighter plane approaching Tehran as before. We heard the explosion but also the anti-aircraft shots, causing confusion. The radio broadcasted a red alarm, urging everyone to seek bunker.

At that time, I was in the first grade of high school. The day after the missile hit Tehran, I went to school, only to find it closed. The following 50 days felt like hell. The war persisted until August 20th, 1988. It was on that day, after nearly eight years, that we finally tasted peace. None of the slogans had been implemented, and a mix of shame and happiness filled the hearts of all of us.
Certainly, the end of every war is the same. To me, war has no winners; in the long term, both sides are losers. We, the people, the families, those who lost loved ones and property, have endured the most precious and beautiful parts of our lives being filled with grief, sadness, and pain.

In today's life, they talk about PTSD: Post-traumatic stress disorder, a fancy term for a mental health condition triggered by terrifying events. During our childhood, youth, and adulthood, who cared about such disorders? Instead, more gasoline was poured on the fire.
During those days, I was so angry and depressed. By the next school year, I started the second grade of high school, and the only difference from the year before was no more war! I'll never forget the day when Khomeini and his son appeared on television. He sat in silence, no longer the verbal nightingale. He had continued the war for 8 years, promising to free Karbala and the Al-Aqsa Mosque, but it seems there was a significant misunderstanding , misinformation, or just a big lie.That was it! He stopped talking. His son Ahmad was reading his notes. Oh yeah! Accepting the cease-fire is like drinking the poison cup for me! This later became a very famous quote.

"Poison cup!" That was the phrase! Eight years of war, hundreds of thousands killed and injured, countless civilians dead, women and children losing husbands and fathers. Trillions of dollars in economic damage, billions lost in sanctions, and he didn't even feel sorry. "Drinking the poison cup!" That was the worst phrase ever.

At the end of his message, he left the door open for further discussion on mortality, stating:

In light of the opinions of all the political and military experts at the country's highest level, whom I trust in their commitment, sincerity, and honesty, I have agreed to accept the resolution and ceasefire. O God, keep this record and book of martyrdom open to the eager, and do not deprive us of reaching it. O God, our country and our people are still at the beginning of the struggle and in need of the torch of martyrdom; be yourself the guardian of this radiant light.

It saddens me to consistently hear the assertion that some intellectuals or the general public insist on believing and saying that Khomeini was instated by the West. Why not acknowledge the reality? The population that fervently supported Khomeini's leadership was genuine. The crowd that mourned his passing was real. Their existence mirrors the misunderstandings and misguided beliefs of a nation at a specific point in time. For instance, why did no one follow Sadiq Hedayat and instead brand him an apostate? Comparing it to suggesting Hitler was brought in by foreigners, at a certain historical juncture, the German mindset gave rise to this tragic chapter. Overlooking the root cause of a problem doesn't resolve it, akin to claiming the West brought about the Taliban.

Without the internal inclination and allure within a society and the depth of a nation's beliefs, it's implausible for such a faction to govern. They are not extraterrestrial beings; they have emerged from the midst of these people and their thoughts. Everyone, willingly or unwillingly, harbors a Supreme Leader or an Amir al-Mu'minin in the depths of their heart and mind; provide it with a fertile ground, and it will manifest itself. Prejudice, a desire for paradise, false beliefs, a thirst for superiority, control over women and children, and numerous other factors can contribute to embracing this ideology and system.

The West may spotlight an issue, topic, belief, or group at a specific moment, but embracing it is entirely your choice, contingent on your understanding and logic in confronting that thought and faction. Only evading responsibility and shunning acceptance hinder the acknowledgment of reality and the resolution of problems.

I recall, 34 years ago, the first time I read George Orwell's novel "Animal Farm." At the beginning of the book, on the first page, he referred to it as "A fairy story." Unfortunately, our generation experienced every line of this story in real life and the actual world. It's an incredible narrative that remains timeless and continuously relevant.

Even the windmill project, initially planned by Snowball and opposed by Napoleon, is part of this remarkable tale. Later, Napoleon, having ousted Snowball, decided to undertake the windmill construction to claim credit for himself. He allocated the entire budget and effort to the project, reducing the standard of living and food, imposing more work and effort on the public.

Even at the end of the story, when the pigs were paraded out with whips, flaunting their power to the animals—reminiscent of our pigs staging their own spectacle with cruise missiles.
The anger, frustration, and post-war anxiety that I reflect on now were the things we suffered from and never fully recovered. Who was contemplating such matters at that time?

In 1989, I was in the second grade of high school, and during one of the PE classes, a few friends and I stayed in the classroom to practice Taekwondo. We had a great time together, and during the break, one of my friends had a sticker of Sylvester Stallone, featuring a photo from one of the Rocky movies with a gun in his hand. He stuck it in the center of the blackboard. Another friend removed it and placed it on a picture of Khomeini, right on top of the blackboard in the middle of his turban.

I knew it could be a bad mistake, so I took it and he insisted to leave it there. When I saw his persistence, I stuck it back, but this time on the lower corner of Khomeini's photo, mentioning that Stallone is now one of his bodyguards, making it less problematic.

After the PE class, we headed to lunch in the school dining hall and forgot to remove the sticker. When we returned to the last class, a geography class, I never forgot what happened. Suddenly, one of the radical students saw the Sylvester Stallone sticker beside Khomeini's photo and made a big deal out of it. The teacher suggested taking it off, but he insisted, claiming it was an insult to their leader and Imam. A group of them left the class with Khomeini's photo and headed to the principal's office.

The school principal, Mr. Mahmodi, a two-faced and opportunistic person, came to our class and asked who did it. A schoolmaster suggested it wasn't a big deal and could be taken off, but Mr. Mahmodi got angry, stating it was a significant insult to the Deputy Imam of Time. He insisted that whoever did it must be punished and expelled from school.

He seized the moment to showcase his loyalty and beliefs, hoping to secure a better position in the Ministry of Education. He was one of those individuals who did nothing for the country but everything to gain more benefits from the system. I knew him well; I witnessed how he conducted himself when alone in his office, especially with young mothers or sisters of students, flattering and flirting them, particularly the younger ones.

And now he is in charge. Right away, he called the Department of Education, Region 14, and the intelligence office based there, informing them about what happened in our school district. They arrived at an unbelievable speed, faster than I've ever seen even with an ambulance or firefighter presence.

"Oh, national security is in danger!" They arrived with a few cars, shut down the school, gathered the entire class, and asked our class representative to show the list of students present during the physical education hours. Unfortunately, my name was on that list.

The school principal offered his office for their use as an investigation and inspection room. They called each student from the list one by one, beating them as much as they could before starting the questioning.

I remember when I entered, one of the guys said, "Heard that you're a tough guy and the Taekwondo guy," and he kicked me in the stomach. Imagine an adult kicking a 16-year-old teenager in the stomach and slapping your face with those heavy hands. You couldn't even defend yourself because they were in power, and their holy Imam was offended by a small Rocky sticker beside his photo.
They had the right to do anything – hitting you, expulsion from school, hindering your path to university or employment, and potentially ruining your life. The guy even threatened to send me to the infamous political prison, Evin.

So when the other guys on the list received the first hit, they all blamed me! Imagine, even the guy who stuck the sticker on Khomeini's photo right in front of his turban.

The boy who brought the Rocky sticker was expelled from school, and now I was considered the criminal. They barred me from attending classes for three months, making me stand in the corridor in front of the school administrator's office as an example to everyone that wrongdoing leads to punishment and suffering.

During this time, they sent me to the Department of Education, District 14, Tehran, marking the beginning of another chain of investigations. Like a scene from a Hollywood movie, the investigation took place upstairs in a room with a single light bulb hanging from the ceiling above a table. Three imposing figures, Hezbollah-style long beards and collared shirts, with rosaries in their hands, questioned me. They began by asking which political group I was working for, and so on.

I insisted that I truly didn't understand what they were talking about. It was a mistake and just a foolish joke among a few teenagers; that was all. However, the guy persisted, claiming I must have been working for one of those political groups.

I maintained my innocence, stating I really didn't know what he meant. The other guy then questioned me about why I didn't believe in Imam Khomeini.

Wow! They really wanted to put words in your mouth and extract something from you! One of them claimed, "Imam Khomeini is like Imam Ali, the first Shia Holy Imam, and his government is similar to him. This government represents justice and is the rule of Ali!"

Upon hearing that, I expressed disbelief, stating that I couldn't accept it. As far as I knew, Imam Ali was kind to orphans, unlike the three of you, big and useless, sitting here questioning me and resorting to torture and slapping my face. My father was killed on the front lines of war to save the country, and we lost our home, living in a difficult area. Yet, here you are, talking about justice and the rule of Imam Ali. It makes me question everything I've heard and read about Imam Ali.

Finally, after a few months, which felt like seasons, they granted me permission to return to classes at school. However, a few weeks later, at the end of the school year and final exams, on Sunday, June 4, 1989, at 7 am, I turned on the radio and heard the news that Khomeini had passed away.

God's supposed rival died! This was the first thought I had upon hearing the news. That was undoubtedly the happiest moment of my life; the guy I had been confronting for disrespecting him was now gone. My mom was surprised because she didn't know what was happening to me; I never told her about school incidents to avoid upsetting her. She already had a lot on her plate. Recently, after 35 years, I shared with her what happened in that year at school. Those days coincided with the last months of my mother's pregnancy. After a few years of my father's death, she was forced to remarry due to the abnormal behaviour of society.
The marriage ended in failure, resulting in another brother for us, which added to my mother's existing responsibilities.

I remember afterward when I confronted Mr. Mahmody, telling him about what happened to his god. I questioned why he died, emphasizing the difference between my god, who never dies, and his.

I've always wanted to send a letter to Sylvester Stallone, sharing my story about what happened because of his Rocky sticker.
So, yeah, I studied hard despite the difficulties and hard times they threw at me. Despite the promised discipline grade reduction and the challenges, I finished that grade, collected my files and documents, and changed my school. Finally, I completed high school, earned my diploma, and gained admission to a university in Tehran.

During those years, I contemplated immigration and leaving the country. The first book I bought was about immigrating to Canada, but I realized it was difficult and required more money. Ultimately, I decided to go to Austria with a friend whose brother lived there. However, my mom disagreed with my decision. Deep down, I didn't want to leave them alone in that high-crime area. I even suggested we go together even as refugees, but my mom was too prideful to apply for asylum.

Days were tough; I bought a Kawasaki motorcycle to commute to university, but the risk of theft added pressure. We had to carry the bike up four flights of stairs daily. After a year, we gave up on the bike and decided to buy a car to work as an Uber driver and for commuting to university. Unfortunately, the guy we trusted sold us a two-door Hillman Avenger, painted and rebuilt after a heavy accident, which we discovered later.
Working with the car proved challenging due to its two-door design. Passengers found it amusing when one wanted to exit before the other. It didn't work well, prompting me to reconsider my transportation options.

On the other hand, because it was a poorly rebuilt vehicle, every specific part of the car was damaged, and the new spare parts were not available in the market. Once, while heading from Qazvin to Tehran, we deviated from the road due to a hole on the highway and flipped the car. We were all in the car with my grandma and mom, and people on the road thought we were all dead. They came to help, rolled up the car, and fortunately, we were all okay, but everyone was scared. We drove back at a low speed to our home, which took a few long hours. After that, I obtained a loan from the university, fixed that scary car, sold it, and got rid of it.

I promised myself never to buy an old car again unless it's a new one!

Our forgotten future in this overlooked society was shaped with various trapped pains that have never been relieved. The Islamic revolution, right in the 20th century, post-revolution trauma, an 8-year-long war surpassing each world war, post-wartime economic collapse and corruption, ideological changes forcing the country against progress and civilization, acting like a black hole, inflation, and shifting social values and moralities!

Perhaps we are the most schizophrenic society globally, living in antithesis. Even the country names reflect this antithesis, such as the Islamic Republic of Iran. It's impossible to be Islamic and a republic simultaneously, as they are opposed to each other. It's easier to be either Islamic or a Republic; these two resist each other, wasting energy and costs, hindering our progress. Even in prayer, we are unsure if we pray to God for our needs or expect blessings from Imams like Ali and Hussien.

In theory, we declare that God is the only one, but in practice, we associate partners with Him! This antithesis implies a form of psychosis.

Our nation is divided into three categories:

- Some people live in the pre-Islam era, staunch supporters of Cyrus, still residing in Persepolis.
- The largest group lives in the early days of Islam, stuck in the alleys of Medina.
- A very small group seeks democracy in today's world.

This small group has been advocating for democracy for at least the last hundred years. However, the resistance from the two other groups, one stuck in 1400 years ago and the other in 2500 years ago, prevents them from embracing change and addressing today's life problems, keeping them trapped in limbo.
This behavior and psychosis are comparable to a person insisting on being the first to pass through an entrance door but refusing to yield when driving, creating a contradiction.

We have consistently lived in a crisis, and it appears to be the government's duty to perpetuate this crisis for its own benefit.

Even the late Malek o' Shoara Bahar, one of Iran's great contemporary poets and a fighter of the constitutional era, expressed disappointment when he saw no change in Damavand's poetry after the constitutional revolution. He implored the volcano to destroy the city of oppression and corruption with its fires.

Today's highly complex world cannot be governed by the superstitions and legends of thousands of years ago. A modern world requires a modern mind; this is our challenge.
For instance, in the 1979 revolution against the Shah's dictatorship, despite the initial push for democracy, the election of an Islamic government led by the mullahs resulted in a transfer of power from one dictator to another, without achieving true democracy.

Attempting to be present in two places simultaneously, both in this world and the other world, is impossible.
If you are eager to become a martyr, you might struggle to drive responsibly, respect laws, and prioritize safety for yourself and others. This perspective suggests the development of a culture of martyrdom in a society where life is viewed as meaningless and worthless.

In the dark era of religious rule, everything was a problem - listening to music, having a video player, a satellite antenna, even the internet! We suffered under the religious government for every specific thing.

I'll never forget the day when, after our lecture at the faculty, a few friends and I headed to Saei Park on Valiasr Street in Tehran to play badminton at a professional level. A girl and her mother passed by, and the girl enjoyed watching our game. She asked her mother to inquire if she could join us. When she sought permission, we agreed.

I recall my friend giving his racket to the girl, saying, "Play with Mohammad." However, shortly after we started playing, the Islamic police attacked the park and stopped us!

Anticipating their arrival, I advised the girl and her mom to run away and leave the scene. We ended up in a fight with the officers, got arrested, and were taken to the morality police station. It was just a normal day for us as youngsters. Eventually, we pledged and signed not to make such a mistake again.

Music was also a problem! Even at weddings, in every wedding, for ourselves and others, we always encountered Islamic police and their reminders to stop the music. Even if you call the police for an emergency situation like a robbery, they will never show up that fast.

The video player was a problem too. I remember when I wanted to buy a video player, I found a guy who knew another person that could provide a video player, like drug dealers! I wanted a specific brand, Aiwa, and paid for it, but they gave me a Toshiba. We had to wrap it in a sack and take it home without looking at it.

satellite antenna was challenging too, it was banned by the government from the first day, learning an advanced language required access to BBC and CNN networks. In one of Tehran's neighborhoods, my brother found a secret satellite dealer. We decided to pick it up in the evening using a motorcycle. Carrying a large bag, we went to the dealer's house. Unfortunately, small dish sizes were sold out, and only large ones remained. My brother had thrown all components like the receiver, LNB, stand, etc., into the bag, but the dish didn't fit. The dealer asked where we had parked our car, and we replied, "In the street next to a tree!" He helped us bring the items down, saying, "Open the back trunk quickly to put it in." As he found out we came with a bike, he nearly passed out from fear and said, "Just leave quickly!" We rode on the motorcycle with the large dish and bag against the direction of the street, hoping to escape if caught by the police.

In short, despite the difficulties, we reached home. My wife, upon seeing the dish, said, "You are crazy!" I replied, "No, we got stuck in this country, which is a madhouse!" The painful part was that we spent half the satellite's price on covering it up on our balcony. Internet, from the very first day, was a huge problem and challenge. Why wouldn't it be?

And sometimes, when I feel mentally exhausted and think I can't do anything more, in retrospect, I believe I give myself the right to be tired.

Finally, I graduated from the university. I recall one of the last lectures before the final exams, where the lecturer asked why, as graduating students, we were so sad. We all shared the same answer – we saw no horizon and no future.

Desperately seeking a job, I found no opportunities wherever I went. Without the funds to start my own business, I refrained from pursuing any governmental job. Nearly a year later, I secured an interview at the Red Crescent Society in Tehran due to its rehabilitation center.

After six months, I received a call for the final interview, an ideological selection by members of the unique Hezbollah group present in government organization offices, including the Red Crescent Society. They rigorously questioned me about beliefs, ideology, and Islamic knowledge. Towards the end, one of them placed the Quran in front of me, asking me to read any page. Opting to recite from memory, I began Surah Al-Waqi'ah, leaving them struggling to follow. A year later, I learned that one of the interviewers was engaged in inappropriate behavior with a colleague.I heard the guy that was testing my knowledge about Islam and god having a sex in same place and same room which questioning me , with one of his female colleagues!

Receiving my first payslip, I was dismayed to find it equivalent to $27 American dollar per month. Despite living in one of the world's richest countries, my dreams of a prosperous future were shattered. The same position in countries around the Persian Gulf paid $1335 American dollar per month at that time.

In a moment of frustration, during Muharram and Imam Hussein ceremony days, I gathered some colleagues to discuss the low salary and high living expenses. However, their concerns were forgotten when someone announced the distribution of free and blessed syrup outside, believed to promote health and healing. They hastily abandoned discussions about their rights and salary, rushing for the holy syrup.

They chose to work in different jobs instead of asking for more pay, opting for a peaceful way to earn money and avoiding confrontation, with the goal of at least receiving a proper minimum wage. The transportation cost exceeded our salary.

Managers and officials with the ugliest thoughts and behavior were selected, turning my hope for reform into despair.
Imagine, after a few years, the Master's degree program in our field began at the University of Rehabilitation Sciences and Welfare in Tehran. I got accepted to attend the course for very first time, but to punish me, they reduced my salary and cut off my technical allowance.

At that time, my salary was around $50 per month, and they deducted $15 per month from it. Instead of supporting my education, they punished me.

Upon earning my Master's degree, they only increased my salary by $10 a month, still not compensating for the amount they deducted earlier.

The thought of leaving the country consumed me, and I contemplated it almost every moment of the day and night. I tried everything, including opening a clinic twice as a partnership, but couldn't continue due to cash constraints. Obtaining a bank loan required a favoritism, and the lack of insurance support meant disabled people couldn't afford expenses. I couldn't bring myself to take money from disabled individuals.
At times, I directed disabled individuals to the Red Crescent Rehabilitation Center, asking my social worker friend to provide them with the maximum discount.

This approach was detrimental to the private business, making it unsustainable for me to continue working.
The farther we progressed, the more challenging it became to stay in that place and work within that system.
I remember that, through collaboration with a charity association in North America, we imported high-quality wheelchairs from South Korea and provided them for free to disabled individuals. Initially, we distributed the wheelchairs together, but once they trusted us, they solely sent the wheelchairs for us to distribute. However, interference came from the president of Red Crescent, who wanted to reserve some wheelchairs for friends and family and we were forced to stop the distribution of the wheelchairs.
He was elected by Khatami, touted as a reformist, and this group was seen as a hopeful force for the country.

I even collaborated with the medical commission to determine the percentage of physical disability of veterans for a while in Red Crescent. It was painful to witness young men, injured in the war, expressing a specific desire to seek medical treatment and rehabilitation abroad. In the midst of evaluation and examination, they would call and instruct me to convey that they could provide the necessary services in the country, although I knew we lacked the required equipment to do it in the country. It was disheartening to deceive those who served the country and work in an atmosphere tainted by embezzlement among officials.
Every day, the idea of leaving and immigrating to other countries grew in my mind. I longed to distance myself from such situations and be in a place where such concerns didn't occupy my thoughts, allowing me to focus solely on work.
There is nothing worse than living in a country that has all the potentials but you cannot succeed because everything is based on theft; the axis of the country revolves around theft.
Everything is arranged in a way that suggests you should be a thief; if you're not a thief, life's affairs won't progress! The more time passed, the more I understood the true meaning of this verse which says:

In the land where I was planted, the beautiful flower was nothing but a thorn.
Depravity and debauchery, regret was not a shame for anyone.

The one who was not affected by this shame is sad and miserable.

In the Iranian governmental structure, the system is designed in a way that you either have to be a thief or life becomes difficult for you if you're not a thief.
Maybe in other parts of the world, particularly in countries with proper governance, someone might be inclined towards theft for more wealth and capital. However, it's no longer acceptable to resort to theft to maintain a normal or ordinary life in a prosperous country! The longing for a simple life, where you work and live in good health.Unfortunately, the Iranian system is designed as a form of internal imperialism. Internationally, it remains unchanged,

regardless of the regime – whether Shah or Islamic – both engage in embezzlement, diverting funds abroad. It operates like a rigged matrix, perpetuating poverty or wealth. Breaking out of poverty seems nearly impossible unless one compromises morals and conforms to the system's expectations.

We do have a serious problem with wages and income and unemployment as Michael Axworthy said in the book of iran Empire of the Mind (p 253-255); *Tehran in 1970s was a strange place, many wealthy to a degree most Europeans could only dream of, live hard by poor people poorer than could be seen anywhere in western Europe.*
The young men of south Tehran, newly- arrived from traditional communities in countryside, either with no job or with only poorly-paid jobs, with little prospect of being able afford to marry or support a family for some years, saw(if they took a bus or taxi uptown) pretty young middle-class women sashaying up and down the street, flush with money, unaccompanied or with girlfriends, dressed in revealing western fashions, flaunting their freedom, money, beauty and (from a certain point of view) immortality. On hoarding, garish depictions of half- dressed women advertised the latest films. Status and the lack of it, is not just about money—it is also about sex and desire.

Tehran was a place of aspiration, but in the late ' 70s it became a place of resentment, frustrated desire and frustrated aspirations for many.
And this class-based gap continued permanently, deepening even further.In our youth during the postwar era, the conditions were dire, and hope seemed elusive for my future. If I had money to invest, there might be possibilities; however, without capital and funds in a country like Iran, progress seems impossible.

I remember computers were very expensive at the time. Despite this, I bought a fax machine with my savings and began corresponding and sending applications to foreign countries. I was eager to leave the country. Even when I sent a letter to a clinic in Yemen, they replied, stating they couldn't afford my salary; This was before the crisis in Yemen.

Since I turned 18, my favorite countries were somehow the US and Canada , but I lacked the funds to apply. I was searching for a country where I could work and apply for immigration in Canada or the US. For about a year, I was contemplating on leaving. At times, I took a leave of absence from work and visited embassies, such as Kuwait, Qatar, Saudi Arabia.

In the end, a group from Jordan, including the president and dean of the University of Jordan, visited our office in Tehran to seek scientific members for the new department and program at their university. Subsequently, they sent me an invitation, and I applied to join them. During those days, without internet finding information about a country like Jordan was challenging.

I even visited Tehran book centers like Khyaban Daneshgah, but couldn't find any books about Jordan. I also checked the foreign ministry book shop, but there was no information available on Jordan.
Even when I received the letter, which served as a kind of visa from the internal affairs of Jordan, I was unsure about the next steps. I searched for the Jordan embassy, initially finding a location close to my office in north Tehran. However, they had recently moved.

When I called the foreign affairs office in Tehran for information on the new embassy address, they were unhelpful. Eventually, I found their new office in Shahrak-e Gharb, rang the bell, and someone behind the metal gate asked about my purpose.

After showing the letter, I inquired about any necessary actions, like applying for a visa, but was told it was permission, and I could proceed as is.

The next day, I returned to my office in Tehran and requested a two-year leave without pay. Unfortunately, they took advantage of the situation and didn't agree to my request for unpaid leave.

I had about two months of leave, and I applied for it. I borrowed money from my mom and my wife's aunt. Since there was no direct flight from Tehran to Amman due to political tensions, I had to take a more expensive option and bought a ticket with Emirates Airlines, costing me about $400 US dollar, which was half the amount of money that I borrowed. It was in March, close to Nowruz, and leaving my family – my wife and 3-year-old son – behind was very difficult for me.

It was a challenging time as they didn't grant me leave, and I was unaware of the new country, my contract, and my situation, making it a vulnerable period. You never know what challenges you might encounter, and the fear of returning home jobless loomed.
In an attempt to prepare, I went to Jomhouri street in Tehran to buy some US dollars from a dollar dealer. With the borrowed money, I could only manage to purchase $400 US dollars (the other half of money that I borrowed).Unable to find Jordanian currency in Tehran, I had no clue about its value.

I worked until the last day in the office and bid farewell to everyone, including my colleagues and students. However, the most challenging part was saying goodbye to my family—my mom, wife, little kid, and siblings.

Despite the difficulty, it was the moment I had been anticipating almost every day for the past year.

My flight departed early morning from Tehran to Dubai, followed by a long layover before reaching Amman. A friend offered me a ride to the airport, which I accepted to avoid inconveniencing everyone with a farewell trip. To lighten my luggage, I opted to bring along many books and booklets instead of personal items like cooking supplies, food, and clothing.

Another concerning factor was the tension between the US and Iraq at that time, and Jordan shared a border with Iraq. The uncertainty of what might unfold was worrisome, especially having just emerged from one war and not wanting to be caught in another conflict. The US-Iraq war took place on March 20, 2003, and by that time, I was already in Jordan. The night before my departure, I sent a fax to the administration office, informing them of my arrival at the airport the following evening. This was the only action I could take as I had little information about the work and accommodation in Jordan.

The only request from my wife was to acquire a cell phone for communication. That early morning, I bid farewell to my family, and a friend dropped me off at the airport, marking the beginning of my journey into the unknown future ahead.

2
Jordan

Finally, I reached Queen Alia International Airport in Amman. It was entirely different from Dubai Airport, and it was evident that Jordan is a less affluent country compared to the Emirates. The only thing that mattered to me was starting my journey to the final destination. As I navigated through arrival and immigration, there was heightened sensitivity towards Iranian nationals due to security concerns, given Jordan's strategic location on the border with Israel.

The downside of the Iranian regime is that it not only makes life difficult for honest people within the country but also damages our foreign relations with its ill-advised actions. It requires considerable effort and courage to prove that individuals like me seek an honest life and want no part in their misconduct. After the questioning, I paid $25, and they stamped my passport, along with an additional stamp indicating a visit to the nearest police station within two weeks, a requirement due to my temporary visa and the fact that I was with an Iranian national.

Fortunately, I met the guy sent by the university to pick me up at the airport because they received my fax beforehand.

At the airport, they charged me in US dollars, and I wasn't aware of the local currency's value yet. The guy, despite his limited English, managed to have a conversation with me. Another positive aspect was that he handed me the key to an apartment unit upon arriving at the university campus. As I entered the unit, I noticed the worn-out furniture. Almost everything was old, broken, and dusty. However, I knew I wasn't there for the furnishings; I already had those back home. Unfortunately, that didn't solve my problem.

I was incredibly tired, having not slept in the last few nights before leaving my country. Upon arrival, I barely paid attention to anything and immediately went to bed.
Fortunately, I arrived on a Friday evening, and Saturday was a weekend in Jordan. Unlike Iran, where the weekend was Thursday and Friday, here it was Friday and Saturday.

I woke up on Saturday morning at 11, feeling hungry with nothing to eat. After getting dressed, I left the apartment in search of food. Having spent $25 USD at the airport for a visa, I now had $375 out of my initial $400. I promised my wife to get a cell phone, so I went to find one and a contact number to stay in touch. Most shops around the university were closed, but eventually, I found a mobile shop with used cell phones. I purchased a Nokia 3210, a prepaid SIM card, and a charge card, spending JD110 (Jordanian dinar). I discovered that at that time, $100 USD was equivalent to 70 Jordanian dinars.

It was shocking to me! I spent $157 USD out of the $375 USD, leaving me with just $218 USD. I used the money to buy food, bread, a frypan, a spoon, a glass, and a small kettle. It made me realize how quickly the money dwindled, considering I had a lot of expenses ahead.
To add to the challenge, there was no money exchange service to transfer money between Jordan and Iran, creating another problem. However, that day, I managed to call my wife and give her my number. Surprisingly, it was more expensive to call from Jordan, so she ended up calling me more from Iran.

On Sunday, I visited the administration and human resources department to sign the contract.
I never forgot the face of that guy who was the head of the human resources department. He was a middle-aged man with a strange personality, making it very hard to read his face. His large desk was close to the window, and there was a big sign with his name written in Arabic. He had a peculiar way of laughing and was a chain smoker with an ashtray full of cigarette butts. He is one of those people I never want to see in my life again. He handed me the contract to sign, and before signing, I inquired about the visa for my family. He burst into loud laughter and replied, "What about your family?" I explained that they needed visas, and he responded, "Not now. By the way, most lecturers here live alone with no family."

I was angry when I heard that, especially with that expression on his face. He was seated behind the desk. I recall standing there, tossing the contract towards him, retrieving the ticket from my pocket, and declaring, I was not going to sign the contract. I had a round-trip ticket to go back. I left the office, firm in my decision.

As I was about to leave Jordan, the faculty dean called my cell phone, seemingly informed by that guy about everything.
I explained that if they wouldn't grant a visa to my family, I couldn't stay.
I was resolute. The dean assured me he would take action, mentioning he spoke to the university president, guaranteeing that my family would receive the visa. He urged me to return and sign the contract.

After that phone call, I returned to the human resources manager's office and signed the contract. One downside of Jordan was that they charged you for everything, sometimes even double or triple, depending on the person in charge. Unfortunately, their hands were often free to accept bribes and money from foreigners.
Sometimes, during the work permits and visa application process, they intentionally introduce delays, blaming you for submitting documents late. They then demanded additional money as a penalty, and the officials in charge switched to speaking in Arabic, and pretended not to understand English.

Nevertheless, they provided me with a list of requirements for employment, including a medical test, HIV test, work permit fees, and visa fees. The costs were substantial, for instance, the work permit set me back 360 Jordanian dinars, and strangely, it needed renewal every semester. Even the requirement for an HIV test seemed like exploitation and taking advantage of foreign staff.

So, I had to ask one of my colleagues to lend me some money. I borrowed 500 Dinars to cover this payment. After the first month of starting, I expected to receive my salary and repay my colleague, but they didn't pay me. I went to the administration to inquire about the month and a half delay after starting my job as a full-time lecturer. They informed me that I needed to go to the intelligence service office, handing me a piece of desktop calendar paper with the address in Arabic.

They emphasized that I must be there at a specific time, stating that failure to attend would result in a delay in receiving my salary. Perplexed, I canceled my lecture on that day and took a taxi to the secret service office located at Eighth Circle (Eighth Roundabout).

I was torn between deciding whether to go or not. If I didn't go, I wouldn't receive a salary and couldn't repay the borrowed money, forcing me to leave Jordan. On the other hand, I didn't want to go back and appear like a loser in front of everyone. It seemed disrespectful to put myself in that position and face questioning.
The situation was challenging; I needed the job, and they needed an educated lecturer with professional skills, a rare specialty in the Middle East at the time. They had explored hiring from other countries but couldn't afford their salaries and benefits.

Now they were taking advantage of us! On the other hand, I understand their concern about knowing someone from a country known for causing trouble. After carefully weighing the pros and cons and considering all possible options, I decided to go there.

When I hailed a taxi on the street and provided the address, the driver, familiar with the area, mentioned it was the Mokhaberat, meaning the intelligent service office. "Exactly," I replied. He dropped me off at a vast open area. At the entrance gate, a small windowless building stood. Speaking to the officer at the gate, he recognized my name on the list, handed me a red badge – a color used for countries like Iran, Iraq, Syria, and others. He directed me to sit on one of the chairs, all facing the wall.

I sat there for a while, and as more people arrived for the interview, they called names one by one. We were instructed to board a mini-bus, creating a quiet atmosphere as we entered a vast, flat area. After a few minutes, we arrived at a large, newly constructed building designed for this purpose. Upon entering, we were directed to the reception, where our identities were checked. Based on the color of our badges, they divided and sent us to different waiting rooms.

Once again, I sat for an extended period, approximately two hours or more. Eventually, an officer came, called my name, and led me upstairs. As we walked, we reached a narrow corridor with chairs facing the wall, where he instructed me to sit and wait once more.

I sat there for a while, and eventually, another officer arrived, checked my name, and instructed me to follow him to the end of the corridor, leading to an interrogation room. Upon entering, the room triggered memories of a similar setting during my second year of high school. It mirrored the past – no windows, three desks, and a chair.

I was directed to sit, with two other individuals entering the room and taking their places behind desks. Two of them proceeded to question me, while the third documented my answers.
The interrogation covered various topics, including my identity, connections, and any interactions with the Iranian embassy and its diplomats.

I responded patiently and honestly. After over an hour of questioning, they concluded, and, surprisingly, the officer apologized for taking my time and wished me a great day.
In contrast, during high school, there was no such acknowledgment after the interrogation.

Anyhow, I left that building, and the bus transported us back to the main gate. After leaving the area, I took a taxi and returned to the university. In the afternoon, the administration office called, informing me that I could go to the bank to collect my salary, which they had deposited into my account.

This was good news for me as, after a prolonged period of work, I could finally repay the borrowed money. The days passed in anticipation. Each day, I visited the administration office, inquiring about my family visa. Unfortunately, the response remained consistent: "Wait, it's in process," and so on.

Somehow, I sensed a lack of cooperation from the personnel in administration and Human Resources. They often shifted blame onto the Ministry of Interior, both internally and externally.

He could be looking for bribes; I really didn't know, but I never stopped following up and asking him. At the end of the semester, after we finished lectures and exams, I decided to go back home for vacation and visit my family. I hoped I could obtain the visa easily, but things never worked out smoothly for me. I went to Tehran and continued asking for the visa, hoping to secure it and purchase tickets for my family to join me there.

The day before my vacation ended, as I started packing my luggage, I was disappointed and thought my family's visas had been denied. Considering going back to Jordan, I recall my 3-year-old son packing his belongings, unaware of visa issues. In a moment of despair, a surprise unfolded by day's end. The phone rang, displaying a Jordanian number. Answering, I discovered my colleague had followed up on the visa matter and requested me to turn on the fax machine to receive my family's visas.

That was a fantastic day, and I wish the positive outcome had occurred earlier. Unfortunately, things didn't align with my wishes.

Now, my family has to come alone since circumstances have changed. I provided all necessary details to my wife before flying back to Jordan the next day.

This trip feels different and more reassuring than the first, as I now have a clear direction. Despite losing my job in Iran during the two-month vacation, I know where I'm headed and can focus without worrying about work and family. My request for a two-year leave without pay was denied, leading to my dismissal, but it's a new chapter for me.

It might have altered the trajectory of my life. I firmly believe in not walking backward; if that situation were okay, you wouldn't have decided to move forward and leave. Always recall Kangaroo and Emu; these animals symbolize progress, always moving forward. As a human, I am no less than them.
When you make a decision in your life, it's the best move at that moment, considering the situation. Don't judge yourself later; decisions are made based on the circumstances then.

Sometimes a decision can alter everything in your life and future. Leaving the quiet corner of your life and embracing change isn't always easy. The road can get bumpy, exposing you to experiences that transform you, making you a different person. Hope, disappointment, and more – these are all part of the journey.

At times, you may encounter disrespect and pain, and your reaction becomes crucial. I recall the first time I reached Jordan. During immigration, they stamped my passport, instructing me to contact the nearest police station within two weeks. At the end of the second week, I visited the nearest police station located in the area called Sweileh.

The police station was in a building with a entrance door featuring a few stairs and medium-sized vases on either side. Upon entering, I approached the reception desk and asked one of the officers for guidance. Inside, there were other people, including families from countries like Iraq. I waited in line.

Before my name was called, a young man, seemingly a new officer, proudly expressing his Jordanian identity and having some knowledge of English, approached me.
In front of everyone, he made a silly comment: "After Iraq, it's Iran's turn! America will attack Iran too," and laughed.

I simply looked at him and responded, "Don't worry about me, but I have a question for you: Are you a Muslim?
He responded affirmatively. I said, "Look at these women and children; they are Arabs and Muslims too. Are you truly happy to witness their displacement? Does the Quran teach you to find joy in the suffering of others? Shame on you!"

He fell silent, and another officer advised him to go and stay on the other side. Being abroad exposes you to things you wish you hadn't seen or heard.

In Iran, since after the revolution, leaders always emphasized being the leader of the Muslims worldwide, expressing concern for the oppressed. They consistently spent our money on Muslims globally but neglected us.

Now, in another part of the Muslim world, there's a lack of concern for our troubles, and it's disheartening to see them happy about our difficulties.
Every day living there was a new lesson for me. I encountered different people, from students and colleagues in university to individuals on the street and alleys. The diversity ranged from mosque to pizza shop, kindergarten to library, hospitals, and shopping malls. Engaging in chitchat allowed me to exchange ideas and opinions with various people.
Once I remembered I went to a salon. Having researched the prices beforehand, the young and tall hairdresser, upon realizing I was Iranian, started talking about Shia Muslims, listing their supposed traits. I simply listened, and when the haircut was done, he quoted a price double the initial one - 20 dinars. I gave him only 9 dinars, expressing that I don't care about the differences between Shia and Sunni, but I'm certain they share a common trait: thievery.

It was a valuable opportunity for me, coming from a Shia background, to be in a place where Sunni Muslims reside. This allowed me to make comparisons between them. Observing both positive and negative aspects, I acknowledge that if I had the financial means for Canadian immigration, I might not have chosen Jordan. However, I believe in God's plan; perhaps, he intentionally led me on a detour.

Once I was invited to a wedding party in a city outside Amman called Irbid. It was a Friday, and we left early in the morning by bus, arriving around noon before the Friday prayers began. My friend suggested attending the Friday prayer first before heading to the wedding. An eye-opening experience occurred when I attended a Friday prayer in Irbid.

The Sunni Mullah spoke respectfully about Imams like Ali, Hassan, Hussien, and Prophet Muhammed's daughter, Fatemeh. This contradicted the narrative I had often heard from Shia Mullahs, fostering a new understanding through firsthand experience.
Many events like that occurred, and I witnessed them. Some were quite amusing! As the head of our department in a new faculty with a curriculum requiring revision, plans for a new building were underway.

During a meeting with architects and engineers, tasked with checking the building plans, I emphasized the importance of a central ventilation and dust collector system for the workshop. I suggested a room adjacent to the workshop for this purpose, insisting on changes to the plan.
I vividly recall pointing out adjustments needed, urging them to correct the sketch by erasing a line and drawing a new one further down.
There was a dispute, and they insisted on following the original plan. They claimed that after construction, another team would handle modifications and address any issues. In the end, I questioned myself why I was bothering and said, "Do whatever you want," before leaving the meeting.
Starting something from scratch involves a lot of work, and it's always challenging. Eventually, we decided to establish a temporary workshop at the university.

We located an old building near the transportation and mechanical site and tasked me with creating a plan for its modification.

After furnishing and installing the machinery, during one of the practical lectures held in this new workshop,
Some students expressed concern about the absence of pictures of the Jordanian king, his prince, and his father on the walls. They contacted the office, and the pictures were brought with frames. When they asked me which wall was better to hang them, I replied that I didn't know, but they insisted, and I pointed to a wall. However, they became upset as the wall was close to the door, deeming it disrespectful.

I have experience with this kind of thing, especially during high school, recalling incidents related to hanging Khomeini's picture. I don't believe in displaying pictures everywhere, inside and outside buildings, on streets and in rooms, but in Middle Eastern countries, it's a common practice. Personally, I don't even put my father's picture on my room's wall at home. Now, there's a debate over where to hang these pictures, and I simply said, "Do whatever you want. It's your country and your business. Enjoy!"

There are many other things that, when I compare them with Iran at that time, evoke sadness. For example, the Islamic hijab was freely practiced in Jordan, and relationships between boys and girls were unrestricted in the university. The irony lies in the fact that Islam originated from the Arabs, and yet, today, many suffer from radical religious practices and their consequences.

We've spent significant time on religious rituals and enforcing hijab appearance through police intervention.
During puberty, adolescence, and youth, suppressing girls and boys had negative effects on their future. It occasionally led to emigration or refugee status, fostering stubbornness and deviance among the youth, altering their fate. Restrictions hindered socialization, resulting in significant damage, unsuccessful marriages, and, sometimes divorce.

At that time, a simple SIM card, quite affordable in Jordan (less than 10 bucks), contrasted sharply with Iran, where it cost a thousand bucks.

In Jordan, satellite antennas faced no restrictions; every house had one, and people earned by installing them. In Iran, however, the government banned them, making it illegal, with penalties for possession. Internet access posed challenges, requiring more payment and causing inconvenience. Comparatively, in terms of natural resources and capital, our country couldn't match Jordan.

Once, I visited Albashir Hospital in Amman for a clinical-practical course with students. One of the volunteer patients was a Palestinian below-knee amputee struggling with personal hygiene. It was challenging during the time I took measurements and cast him for a new prosthesis, demonstrating for the students. Despite the difficulties, he was happy with the technique. However, when I finished, he asked about my origin. I said Iran, and he replied, "I never go to Iran because if I go there, I couldn't go to the USA, and I don't want to lose this opportunity." It made me question why we endure national and international struggles for this nation.

I recall when I worked at the Red Crescent Society back home, and they deducted a percentage of our salary to aid Palestinians. I wasn't pleased, questioning why they did it without my permission. Another time in my lecture room, a Palestinian student arrived late, holding coffee in one hand and his girlfriend's hand in the other, attempting to enter humorously. I stopped him, stating that it wasn't allowed due to tardiness. He argued loudly, claiming that in America, people do as they please.

I corrected him, explaining the difference between reality and Hollywood movies. Despite the ongoing crisis in Jerusalem, supporting such behavior with our funds is unacceptable and shameful. Supporting Palestinian by Iranian government causing billions in losses annually, and our youth suffer as a result in Iran.
It may seem that only the negative aspects are expressed here, but it's important to note that I am not attempting to write a travelogue. Instead, I am exploring the factors that led to the main problems in my life and migration.
Since the day of arrival, I have been aware that I must depart from Jordan due to high living expenses, additional charges, including those for work permits and visas purposely delayed and paying for the penalties , leaving me with minimal income.

The cost of flights from Amman to Tehran, coupled with work permit expenses per semester, has depleted my savings, hindering my plan for immigration to Canada. Faced with these challenges, it feels like the end of the world, and achieving my initial goals seems nearly impossible.

In the second year, I found an opportunity to apply for Bahrain, a different country that is closer to Iran and has a direct flight to Tehran. It is on the other side of the Persian Gulf and is economically better and richer than Jordan. I heard there could be a possibility to obtain citizenship in Bahrain. Seeing this potential, I gathered all the required documents, my CV, and copies of my qualifications and certifications. Subsequently, I sent them to Bahrain through one of my Bahraini students.

The position was entirely different; I had to transition from lecturing at the university to a clinical role, which I knew would involve more labor. However, sometimes, for a substantial change and plan, you need to overhaul everything. Even though asking my student was the toughest part, for the sake of my family and a better situation, you must do what is necessary!

If our politicians, past, present, and future, had learned to be flexible, willing to change, and set aside foolish pride, swallowing what is often termed as pride for the sake of the country and the nation, our current situation would be entirely different.
Although migration may seem easy in words, in practice, it is a challenging and weighty process. Every specific move could become a great story later on! After my family arrived in Jordan, we decided to register my 3-year-old son in a nearby kindergarten within the university area, which was a half-hour walk away and conducted classes in Arabic.
I never forgot the first day we left him there; he was so eager to learn in the Iranian kindergarten.
However, in Jordan now, the 3-year-old boy has to attend an Arabic-language kindergarten, and he has no familiarity with the language. My wife's eyes welled up, on the verge of tears. She expressed concern that it could be very challenging for him and might be a big shock. I reassured her, saying a shock at this age is better than a shock in adulthood!

After a few days, we received a call from the kindergarten teacher who spoke a little English and said, "Your son is having trouble in kindergarten, please come over." We rushed there anxiously and stressed, only to find out that the issue was the teacher asking my son to leave his school bag and books on the shelf. He resisted, leading to a verbal exchange where the teacher spoke in Arabic, and my son responded defiantly in Persian.

It was a horrible experience, and my wife cried, but for an immigrant, it's important to be tough and not give up. I remember once when he learned the language and spoke fluently, they called to complain about him talking too much and distracting others. I found it amusing and considered it the best complaint ever!

During the days when he was learning the language, we encouraged him to speak by bribing him with gifts and everything he wanted. It made him happy and more interested in learning.

Days have passed, and I am still seeking a way to leave Jordan. I don't want my immigration journey to conclude here; my thoughts persist as I explore other countries, particularly Canada.

To be honest, one of the toughest things is to find a country with diverse people, culture, capabilities, and especially language, which is a crucial factor to consider. Among all countries, I'm concentrating on those where English is spoken, such as New Zealand, Australia, England, the USA, and Canada.

Among them, I chose Canada. Perhaps it was just a gut feeling, or maybe the United States lacks an immigration system similar to Canada's, with distinct legal classifications for various skilled immigrants at the time.

From other perspectives, these two countries have the most complex relations, and being in either of them exposes you to a whole different world. Towards the end of the third year, my Bahraini friend, who was assisting me in applying for a job at the Ministry of Health in Bahrain, visited me and mentioned that there would be good news soon, with contact expected from Bahrain.

Yes, he was right. In the early days of January 2006, I received a call on my cellular phone that wasn't familiar while I was walking to the faculty. I'll never forget that moment. I answered the call, and it was a friendly and polite person who happened to be the head of the human resource department at the Ministry of Health in Bahrain, delivering the news.

The person provided me with information about the situation and asked for a fax number to send the contract and some forms. As I didn't want to disclose this to my colleagues, I postponed providing the office fax number, stating that I would share it later that day. I walked out onto the street, where numerous print shops were nearby. I entered one and asked for the fax number.

Then, I called the person in Bahrain, providing him with the fax number. He sent everything to me via fax, and after paying at the shop, I left. Once again, a new hope and beginning, restarting the process of gathering all necessary documents, filling out forms, and signing the contract. Paperwork is a crucial and integral part of the process. Following that, I sent the documents to Bahrain via DHL.

Every country has different rules and requirements. Eventually, I received a letter instructing me to undergo a medical test, which I completed without hesitation. This included a chest X-ray, blood test, stool examination, and more. Surprisingly, I managed to complete all tests in a single day. Even when the lab technician suggested doing them later, I pressured myself to finish everything so I could send the results before the DHL office closed at the end of the day. Since it was all done in the private sector, it was somewhat manageable.

Finally, I sent all the reports to the Ministry of Health in Bahrain. A few days later, I received an invitation letter and was supposed to visit the Bahrain embassy in Amman for visa stamping. Upon our visit, the good news was that they stamped the visa on my passport's page gratis! Wow!

This is wonderful! They arranged with Gulf Air airline, and I received my prepaid ticket. However, there was no visa provided for my family, only a temporary three-month visa for me.

I was informed that visas for my family would be issued later. On that day, we visited Gulf Air airline, and I acquired my ticket. Additionally, I purchased tickets for my family.

So, we could travel together halfway to Bahrain, and from there, they would take another flight to Tehran. I disliked being separated from my family again, but unfortunately, I couldn't do anything about it.

We prepared ourselves for another immigration. Over the last three years, we acquired and purchased numerous items for daily living. We gave away most of these belongings, keeping only a selected few, which we sent to Bahrain via cargo. Among the items were dishes and china, gifts from my wife's mother for our wedding, and sadly, we had to part with all of them.

It was mid-March, and my son was in first grade at a private elementary school. We had paid the tuition for the entire year, leading us to contemplate the situation. Although he loved the school, we were considering the importance of time for us. During those days, Ahmadinejad became president in Iran, and every time he spoke, he seemed to create more problems for us!

We weighed the pros and cons of the situation and the world, so we decided to leave. We planned to send my son to school and have him repeat the same grade in Bahrain in the new education calendar. Even though I hadn't received my salary until a few days later, we made the decision to leave.

On the day of departure, early in the morning, I had a clinical lecture at Albashir Hospital in downtown Amman with my students. After finishing the class around noon, during our goodbyes, when the students said, "See you tomorrow," I smiled and replied, "Maybe not!" They didn't quite get it!

I took a taxi, headed home, changed my clothes, and we prepared to leave. Going outside, I called a taxi to take us to the airport. We brought out the suitcases, placed them in the taxi's trunk, and headed to the airport.

Happy for another startup but sad about another separation. When we reached the airport, I disposed of the keys in the trash bin at the main entrance door. Then, we proceeded to the gate, ready for a new adventure!

Never forget that during our 2005 summer vacation in Iran, we made some investments. Facing a shortage of funds to return to Jordan via Emirates airline, we opted for Iran Air tickets to Syria. Our plan was to visit Damascus, take a taxi, and return to Amman. The other day, I obtained the visa from the Syrian embassy in Tehran. I recalled that Iranian Mullahs don't need a visa to travel to Syria, and I found that rather surprising.

So, we flew to Damascus on an old Boeing 747, and the plane was full of passengers with almost no empty seats. Before arriving, I discovered that the flight took longer than what the captain had mentioned. I asked one of the flight attendants why the travel time to Damascus was much longer. She replied, "I don't know; maybe you are mistaken." However, I sensed that something unusual was happening.

Finally, the pilot called for an emergency landing, and all the masks dropped down. It was quite turbulent. In the end, we discovered that one of the wheels wasn't working, so the pilot decided to circle until the fuel tank became empty. Then, the plane underwent an emergency landing, and ultimately, all wheels were deployed as we safely landed in Damascus.

It was a horrible experience, my first flight after years with Iranian Airlines, which, due to the sanctions, saw a decline in quality and safety day by day. Who cares? Arabs call their people Mavaten, meaning citizens, and Westerners also refer to their people as citizens. Yet, I still don't know what our role is as a people—seemingly providing a free ride for the government officials to fulfill their absurd desires!

Anyway, when we landed at Damascus airport, you could see Assad's photo everywhere, but the airport toilets seemed like they were from centuries ago, placed underground.

With all the money and support they received from the Iranian government, where did it go?
So, when we exited the airport, I called a taxi and inquired about the best hotel in Al-Sayyida Zainab. I had heard a lot about Syria and this place, and I just wanted to confirm if it was really as described. Upon arrival, the driver stopped in front of a new building, stating that it was the best hotel in the area. After comparing it with other hotels, I believe it truly was.

It was evening, and the sun had already set. We got a room, placed the suitcases, and went out for dinner and to explore the surroundings. Poverty was evident around the buildings and houses, which were timeworn, even the cars on the street.
As we walked in the bazaar around the Al-Sayyida Zainab area, we observed the unhappiness of the people.
And I'll never forget a few young people who walked near us, overheard our conversation in Farsi, and began swearing. It seems like they blamed Iranians for the situation in their country.

I'll never forget the moment I told my wife that something bad would happen to this country, like a revolution, rebellion, or war. A few years later, when the Arab Spring began in 2011 and revolution unfolded in Syria, I wasn't really surprised to hear about it. Anyway, we took a taxi from the hotel, left Damascus, and headed to Amman. On our way, we saw Assad's photos everywhere, extending to the border of Jordan.
When we reached the border, you could see the difference between the two countries. Even though Jordan wasn't a rich country, it was in better shape compared to Syria. Upon arrival, it felt much better!

3

Bahrain

On our flight to Bahrain, a complex feeling of happiness and sadness arises, and we wonder how long we will stay apart again.
When the plane landed, we walked into the transit corridor together.
After a few minutes, we shared our last hug and goodbye, hoping to be reunited soon. My family continued to the gate, and I proceeded to enter Bahrain. After passing through immigration and collecting my baggage from the carousel, I headed towards the exit door.

This time was a big surprise! My Bahraini friend, whom I knew from Jordan and who helped me apply for the position in Bahrain, was there with his wife. It was a big relief, and I'll never forget the favor he did by leaving Jordan earlier to be there because of me. After greeting, he had another surprise for me: he got a Bahraini SIM card, and later that night, I called my family in Iran and gave them my contact number.
So he dropped me off at the temporary home provided by the Ministry of Health, where I had one week to stay until I found a place to rent.

After an hour, he came back to take me for dinner at an Iranian restaurant in Manama. We drove there, and it was a nice restaurant with a good design and, of course, Indian staff. We enjoyed fresh bread with kebab, which is my favorite meal. I can't imagine how things are different this time; I wish I had come to Bahrain instead of going to Jordan in the first place.

But many things had happened between Iran and Bahrain before that I wasn't aware of until I discovered later on. Due to those problems, I couldn't apply for Bahrain. The reason I am here now is that I had been in Jordan, which is a more geo-strategic area and approved by Jordanian intelligence service agencies. That's why I can work as the only Iranian employed in a governmental job in Bahrain.

The food was delicious, and I especially enjoyed the tea right after dinner. They say it's wrong to have tea immediately after a meal, but who cares! Sometimes, doing the "wrong" thing cheers you up and gives you a good feeling.
After dinner, my friend took me to Babul Bahrain in downtown Manama, a historical place. That night, due to Arba'in, a mourning ceremony was held in that area by Shiites. He wanted to show me that celebration dedicated to Imam Hussein in Manama.

So we walked downtown, witnessed the ceremony, and had tea and sherbet—familiar things we grew up with since childhood in Iran.
It was around midnight, and we decided to go. He had to drop me off at my place and then return to his house.

So we reached my place, and I got out of the car, bidding farewell to my friend as he left. I lingered for a bit until he was gone—a polite habit in Iran.
So when I got to the main door of the building, I found it locked. I knocked, but no one was there to open the door. It was my first night there, and I didn't know anything about the rules.
I had a long day since I left Jordan on that day, and by the next day, I had to start my new job early in the morning. I needed to take a shower, change my clothes, and get some rest—at least lie down. However, I found myself stopped behind the locked door.

My friend had just left, and I was too shy to call him and explain what was going on. I came up with an idea and started to walk down the street, telling myself I might find a hotel to get some rest for tomorrow. Hoping for the best, after a few kilometers, close to the intersection, I saw a hotel sign. I entered the building, approached the reception, and asked for a room for the night.

Luckily, I had my passport and money with me. I paid in cash, using American dollars, but they requested Bahraini dinars. They exchanged the dollars at a good rate, and I paid 20 dinars. This time, I wasn't shocked because I knew that $100 American dollars were equivalent to 35 Bahraini dinars at the time.
I got the key and room number, went upstairs to enter the room. It was late, and I didn't pay attention to the facilities and furniture. I just took a shower and got into bed, still reviewing the day before drifting off to sleep.

Still battling with sleep, I heard the hotel phone ring. Wondering what could be going on, I guessed maybe I forgot my ID card or passport at the front desk. I picked up the phone and answered. A lady on the line asked if I wanted a massage. Perplexed, I said, "Did I ask for a massage?" She replied, "I just offered you," and I responded with a "No, thanks" before hanging up the phone.

A few minutes later, the phone rang again, and I answered. A different voice, a lady, asked the same question, "Do you need a massage, sir?" I replied, "No, thanks," and dropped the phone. I've never had such an experience in any hotel. What is that?
While my mind was preoccupied with the strange phone call, the hotel phone rang again. This time, it was a different lady who spoke both Arabic and English. She asked me if I wanted a lady in my room for company. I replied, "No, thanks!" She got angry and asked, "Where are you coming from?" I answered, "Iran."
I hung up the phone, but this time I unplugged it, causing an interruption. In the end, I managed to sleep for an hour or two that night, and I couldn't help but wonder why I had chosen to stay in that kind of place.
Finally, morning arrived, and I had an appointment with my friend at my place. Since I wasn't there, I preferred to call him early and explain where he could meet me, detailing what happened the previous night when I mentioned the name of the hotel.

He quickly mentioned that it isn't a good place. It seems all the local people know about this place, and I learned my lesson too. Those days weren't like today when you have data on your mobile and can search for everything on Google, read comments, and even book and pay for the hotel using apps.

I went down to meet my friend outside the hotel, and we went to the cafe shop for breakfast. Afterward, we headed to the human resource office in the ministry for some paperwork. We also visited the head of the human resource office, and I recall that my friend brought up what happened to me last night. He laughed loudly and said, "Now you know that we have freedom in Bahrain."

So they gave me the instructions for the medical test, which needed to be done again, and a cheque for my settlement. This was a totally different experience and situation compared to Jordan.

After all, we headed to the hospital department for a visit with the head of the department and an initial tour of the department and staff. So, it was a good day and a good start.

Only those who have experienced living abroad know how important it is to know someone and have someone beside you to help you get settled, especially in the Middle East.

The next step was finding a place to rent. Every day, we checked the local daily newspaper to see the ads for rental properties, and my friend helped me go and visit the places.

I was lucky that he stayed the entire week in Bahrain and even helped me retrieve my stuff from the cargo in the airport area.

My limitation was to find a place that I could walk to work and be around shops for my daily commute until I buy a car. Due to the high temperatures in Persian Gulf countries, you can't live without AC and a car.

The other thing that I quickly discovered I had to consider was the security of the place, not due to theft but because of tensions between Shiites and Sunnis, which was a serious issue. I wasn't aware of this until the early days of my stay in Bahrain when I heard about it.

Luckily, I found an apartment close to the hospital, situated in a diplomatic area where many embassies were located, including the Iranian and American embassies. It was a good and very safe area, and we lived there until our last days in Bahrain.

It was expensive compared to other places, but due to my upbringing and past experiences, I learned one of life's most important lessons: security is our top priority, and we must be willing to invest in it.
So during my first visit, I liked the place and made up my mind. It was a fully furnished apartment with brand new furniture, and the building itself was also new. It had a large balcony, which was unique because it was the only unit in the building with one, somehow due to its design.

The good thing about it was that the building belonged to a big corporation, not an individual, so you could stay there as long as you wanted with fewer headaches compared to a place where the owner lives and wants to control everything. Especially if the owner is mean, then you're in trouble.
It just had a nice guy who was a young man from Bangladesh working there as a watchman, taking care of the property, and even collecting the rents.
So the next day, I went to Manama with my friend to sign the contract, and I paid three months' rent in advance. By the end of the week, my friend arranged for a pickup driver, and I moved to the new apartment.

At least I've sorted out the accommodation and can now focus on the other things that still need sorting out. A new job always requires more energy and effort to ensure that everything is alright, especially in our clinical field where there are different positions with varying levels of social interaction.
Dealing with both a shoemaker and an orthopedic surgeon requires good intentions, which are key factors in this field. On the other hand, there are physically disabled people ranging from those with deformed limbs to those with amputated limbs, each with their own personal capacity.

And everyday life is challenging for them, with different difficulties and varying levels of mental and physical strength. As a therapist, it's crucial to maintain your life balance and be prepared to face these everyday challenges.
Never forget on the first day of my official start, the head of the department, in front of the other staff whose ranks were helpers and technicians, assigned me a simple task: to trim it with a router machine.

My qualifications were higher than his. Just the week before, I was teaching at the university, and I had two Bahraini students from this department in my class. I've trained many students from different countries, from Yemen to Jordan, from Afghanistan to Iraq, Iran, and beyond. And now, look at me!
The person who was a member of the first group accepted for a Master's degree in our field in the very first instance in the Middle East is now being treated like this.

I always said that the greatest asset of all is being born in a good country! If you are born in a good country, you are the luckiest person in the world. With less effort and energy, you can stay in the best place, and your dreams will come true more easily!
Imagine all the effort I put into running that department at Jordan University. They didn't even mention my name in their historical background. Why? The simple answer lies in Iran's conditions and its chosen foreign policy, particularly its approach to dealing with the rest of the world, especially other countries in the region where they seek to export the Islamic revolution.
Due to ignorance, and delusion, wasting our energy and life. Anyway, I did it. I trimmed that piece.

Since I left my home country, I've only been seeking a basic life and have completely forgotten about idealism and dreams. Mostly, I've become the most realistic version of myself, living by the slogan 'another day, another dollar'.
This is the only reason I am here. I chose not to be a thief or hustler and to live with dignity. Of course, you have to pay for that.

The system in Iran wants you to be a thief and a charlatan. Then you're okay. But if you want to be righteous, then even for a very basic life, you have trouble. Having a normal life is the biggest problem in present-day Iran.
In fact, in the rest of the world, even in countries with average economies and incomes, ordinary people don't resort to cheating and stealing for a basic life. I saw in a poor country like Jordan, our faculty mail guy was building his own house, while a professor in Iran has to work extra as an Uber driver with his car to pay his rent and bills!

People normally steal if they want extraordinary things, not for basic necessities. Anyway, I did that job, and he admired me for it. But later on, around noon, when I went for prayer and opened the cabinet in the training room to get a prayer mat, I saw a photo of Khomeini stuck inside the door of the cabinet. Oops!

The problem is here too! Now I understand why some guy asked me earlier which Matam I am going for Aza! Even one of the physiotherapists asked me, and I replied, 'If I wanted to go to Matam, why would I leave the biggest Matam in the entire world (meaning Iran) and come here?

I did some research and found that the problem between the two countries is deeper and worse than I thought. In August 1979, Khomeini sent his representative, Hadi Modaressi, to Bahrain, causing significant trouble and exporting the Islamic revolution to the country. Since then, serious issues have persisted between the two countries, to the extent that they even temporarily halted diplomatic relations.
Yeah, everywhere we go, it seems they've been there before and they've disrupted the atmosphere of our lives, not just in our home country but in every other country, even those far away from us.

Now I find myself in a poisonous mess created by them. People of every nationality, from Western Europe to India and Bangladesh, come to Arab countries to work, save money, gain experience, and then return to their homelands. However, wherever we go, we are constantly faced with difficulties.

I remember that after the first month, the weather started getting hot, and I couldn't continue walking to work; I needed a car. To buy the car, I needed a loan. However, since Ahmadinejad became president, banks in Bahrain stopped giving loans to Iranians.
Finally, I found a broker who could provide a car loan at the last minute because I was working for the government of Bahrain. Even though I couldn't buy the car I initially wanted, I ended up purchasing a car from a company and brand that could provide me with the loan.
Even for the Bahraini driver's license, as an experienced driver, they only give us one chance for the exam and road test.

It is very stressful; if we fail the test, we have to start over, go back to driving school, and spend a lot of time and money until we obtain the Bahraini driver's license.

I totally forgot that war is a blessing! Any nationality can even get a personal loan ten times their salary and invest in their home country to overcome inflation, except for us. Isn't that painful?

Even at the Ministry and hospital, the doctors and surgeons are unhappy with our head of department. They sent someone to me with a message that if you had a Western passport, we would replace you with that guy. They said he made the department like a Matam.
They see my ability and interest in helping, but their hands are tied. It's the story of my life! Yes, I know that very well, but what can I do? I even remember, the Iranian government had a bank in downtown Manama at that time called Future Bank. Even when I asked them for a loan, they didn't give it to me.

I know they are not helping their fellow countrymen. If they were, why should I stay here? This facility is for their own personal use and for developing their ideology in the region because they provide good facilities to Arab citizens.
I was in a position where I provided services to this country, but instead, I received the least benefits due to political issues. On the other hand, the radical Shia don't want me to be there because it proves that the Bahraini government doesn't have a problem with Iranians but with the strategy they have against the Bahraini government, believe me, it's not a good position to be in abroad. But here I am now, and as they say, it is what it is.

The hardest part of life is buffering, a way of avoiding our negative emotions and giving ourselves temporary relief. Buffering hurts us because we believe we need external things to feel better. We stop buffering by acknowledging its cost and become aware of the emotions we are trying to avoid.
But is it possible to keep the external things that result from the actions and decisions of our leaders in order? Of course not.
One of the problems in the Middle East is that people there dig into your soul to uncover your beliefs and then begin to fight you.

Many years ago, my wife and I worked the night shift in downtown Vancouver, from 5 pm to 1 am, and spent mornings searching for jobs related to our field and licenses, among other things. In short, we took the last sky train and bus home at night. Friday nights held many stories, Usually, most people returned from downtown bars. Sometimes, some individuals attributed our tiredness to our drunkenness and hangover. It was a different world; occasionally, you would see someone who had lost control of their limbs due to extreme drunkenness.

One was moving back and forth, one person was grabbing the train handle and pulling upwards, some were sitting next to us and chatting, while another was on the other side vomiting.

But one night, a man approached us and started talking. He asked where we were from and what our names were.

In short, when he realized we were from the Middle East, He said, "My wife is Jewish, and when we went on a trip to Israel, anyone who approached me, before asking my name, inquired about my religion and beliefs. Why are the people of the Middle East like this?"

Well, I was stuck in a difficult situation. I really didn't know what to say or where this discussion would end. All I could think of was, do you know why? Because they can serve you better. That's it! They don't mean anything else!

And what happened on my first day at work in Bahrain. I'll never forget that during prayer time, someone handed me a Turbah or Mohr, which Shia people use for prayer. I was shocked because I had never been in this situation before.

Later, I discovered that the guy was an anti-government activist who had been in jail for a while because they arrested him with a gun years ago. He had a radical mindset, and figures like Khomeini and Khamenei were like gods to him.

It was surprising that he could still work for the government in Bahrain, which was actually a good thing.

The sad part of the story is that he teaches children how to read the Quran and even gives morality lessons.

There was another guy who was a radical Sunni. Since he arrived at work early in the morning, he would turn on the radio and

listen to the Quran at a loud volume straight for 8 hours, and you really get sick of him!
Who does this? Imagine working with handicapped people and back in the workshop having to listen to the Quran for 8 hours straight! He was also anti-American, and during a break, he once got into a fight with me when he found out that I am not anti-Western, specifically America!
And he threatened me, saying, "You shouldn't like America as long as you live and work here!"

And every day at break time, when we all gather together to have tea or a light sandwich, I have to listen to political discussions, but I can't even talk or give my opinion because I don't want to face any consequences. This was my situation for seven and a half years.
After staying in Bahrain, in the summer of 2007, I obtained a visa to attend an international conference in our field, which was held in Vancouver, BC, Canada. I decided to go alone, and the decision was based on the possibility of finding a job and being able to stay in Canada. If I succeeded, my family would join me later.

I arranged everything for that plan, even paying off the car loan and changing the registration. However, in July and August, the travel agent couldn't find a flight with a reasonable price for me. After a two-week wait, they offered me a business class ticket with a significantly increased fee,
which I rejected that offer and switched agencies. This time, I provided guidance to the new agent, explaining that I didn't want to waste time if crossing the Atlantic Ocean wasn't possible. I suggested that crossing the Pacific Ocean might be an alternative route.
Luckily, the guy caught my idea and found a flight with a Pacific route at a reasonable price. However, it was the longest flight I've ever taken, from Bahrain to Hong Kong and then to Vancouver with Cathay Pacific Airline, each flight lasting 13 hours. Nonetheless, it was worth it despite being during the peak season.
I had a plan, but how this plan might work, only God knows. So I left my family again and looked for another possible opportunity. When I arrived at Vancouver airport after that long flight, during

immigration, when the officer asked me, "Are you going to stay here?" I honestly answered, "If I find a legal job offer in my field, why not?"

From the airport, I took the bus and chatted with people about the situation and life here in Vancouver. Even on the first bus, there was an old lady who was a retired nurse. When she found out that I am from Iran, she mentioned that she had been in Iran, specifically in Isfahan, for a while before the 1979 revolution and talked about her experiences and memories in Iran. It was a nice experience for me chatting with people on public transportation. Even though I didn't have exact change for the bus fare, one old lady kindly paid for me. When we arrived at downtown Vancouver, I insisted on paying her back and luckily, we got off the bus at the same stop in front of Seven-Eleven. I changed my 100 dollar bill and paid her back.

I continued walking down the street to find my hotel. It was around 11 am in the morning when suddenly four guys blocked my way. One of them had taken off his t-shirt, revealing some muscles, and led the team in mugging the newcomer, asking for money and threatening me.
I was really tired after that long flight with severe jet lag. After the nice chat on the bus with people, I didn't expect to face this scene right after getting off the bus! But the poor guy doesn't know who I am.
I wasn't shocked because I had never faced fighting with gangsters before, but I was just surprised because I didn't expect it at that time of day in Vancouver! So, I loudly said to the guy, "You're messing with the wrong guy, baby. I could take you all down, but let me know which one of you wants to be first in line?"
How strange life is, that scene took me back years ago when I was 20 years old. It was one of those Ramadan nights. My brother and I were walking to a friend's house for Quran recitation. My brother is 6 years younger than me.
That night, we walked with comfortable sandals because the distance was short. As we walked on the sidewalk beside the building in front of us, in the darkness, I saw lots of cigarette lights, and suddenly my sixth sense told me something was going on here.

And I was right. When we stepped closer, I saw the gangs that I knew. One of them stepped forward, said something bad, and wanted to start a fight.

I hesitated, then grabbed my brother's hand and walked faster. I told him to leave the scene and run to my friend's house to ask for help. There was no chance to send him back home because they had blocked our way back by standing there.

So when I was sure that my brother had left, I made a plan for them. I started to run because I was a Taekwondo player with a black belt, and they were just some junkies who showed power to poor people. My biggest concern that night was my brother, who was also a Taekwondo player, but just a young kid, and they might hurt him.

So I continued my technique of running and stopping. When one of them reached me, I bit him. There were a lot of men to fight with; I wasn't sure, maybe around twenty people.

When you find yourself in this situation, the most important thing is to not allow yourself to be surrounded by them, as one of them might stab you with a knife. Also, you should focus on the stronger person. If you handle that person effectively, the rest will become scared and run away.

Living in Koye Azadi gives you a ton of experience that I never thought would be useful in my first few hours after landing in Vancouver!

So when I left the heavy suitcase with one hand, almost at the level of my shoulder, and took on the stance and guard of fighting, ready to throw that suitcase at the face of the muscle guy, the other gang members understood what was going on. One of them shouted for him to stop, and they grabbed him and ran away, leaving me alone.

Finally, I found the hotel and went to the reception to ask for my reserved room. However, the room was still occupied. They gave me another room for the next two days until mine became available and ready.

I took a hot shower and then lay down for a few hours. I had never experienced such a long flight in my entire life. The longest flight I ever had was to Stockholm, which was around five and a half hours. But this time, I crossed the entire Pacific Ocean, and I truly understood the meaning of jet lag.

By the evening, I got out of the hotel and went for a walk to discover the place where the Congress will be held.
I followed the address, which I had saved in my Google Maps on my laptop. I wrote down the address and the name of the street on paper. Now, you can even see which bus to take. That was quite helpful. Additionally, the hotel started offering free WiFi, which was really useful.
When I walked down the street, I saw the beautiful waterfront and Canada Place, where the congress was being held in the next two days.
I continued walking to Stanley Park, enjoying the amazing view with an ocean perspective. The weather was perfect for a late July evening, which made it impossible to go for a walk in Bahrain at this time of year.

Sometimes in life, you miss the basic things, like walking on the street, drinking water directly from a tap, breathing fresh air, walking in the woods, experiencing rain, etc. These are the basic things that bring real happiness but in Gulf countries, you never have these things. To take a walk, you must drive to the mall, and drinking water from the tap is not possible. There are no woods, rain, or snow.

There are no four seasons over there, only one season: a long, hot summer and a very short spring lasting just a few days!
You can't have everything together. In the Persian Gulf countries, they are rich in oil and money but poor in terms of nature and weather conditions.
Anyway, I spent late July and the entire August in Vancouver. During the congress, I talked with people in the field, even due to a previous arrangement with a guy from Saskatchewan. To find that person, I suggested to one of the officials to install a board for messages and finding friends in the hallway.

Fortunately, they did this task, and a large board was installed, on the top of it, it was written; 'leave your message here.'

I found him and talked with him about the job and the possibility of joining them. It was unpleasant and full of ignorance; he might have been the wrong person to talk to, but at least I tried.

I remember during the congress meeting an Iraqi friend whom I knew from Jordan. He was there and mentioned his plan to stay in Canada rather than returning with their team.

After the congress, I had more time to go around and visit more people and places. I remember there were many events in front of the art gallery in downtown Vancouver, with most of the political events being held there.

One day while I was walking around, I remember seeing some Persian guys demonstrating there. From the famous photo of Rajavi they were hanging, it was clear that they were from the Mojahedin group which is another form of extremism and radical ideology in Iran.

They carried a big, old TV and video player and showed a video about executions in Iran. A lady walked among pedestrians with a long paper in her hand, asking people to sign a petition for human rights in Iran.

When she came to me and asked me to sign, speaking english with Iranian accents, I inquired about the purpose. She replied, "For human rights and to stop executions in Iran!"

I had my opinion too. I asked her about the photos and who the people in them were. She said they were our leaders. Then, I asked her, "Where is your country's flag?"

I said to her, "What's the difference between this and that in Iran? Ideology is ideology, and an idiot is an idiot! Sorry, I can't sign this for you because it's not for the sake of the country, but for the sake of another shit!"

As I left that place and continued walking on the street for a few hours, I eventually returned to the hotel from another direction.

I realized that this group was another radical group with a different ideology that could not tolerate different or opposing views. And they might harm me.
Every day you see something different. The other day, I saw another group gathered there because George Bush was visiting Canada, and they were chanting about war and the NAFTA agreement.
I saw an Iranian community with a booth there and some pamphlets they were giving to people. I went closer to them and started talking. There was a lady who said to me, "Throw away your documents and everything, and stay here. Everybody does that, it means applying for asylum!"

I told her I have all my documents, name, and qualifications, and nobody cared about them. How would throwing them out change anything? But then I asked her a question, and I said, "Please, be honest. Are you really happy here?" I saw tears starting in her eyes, and she said nothing but silence.
I said, "Please, don't mention or offer this to anyone. Being a refugee is not the answer; don't waste it. Please keep this door open for people who truly need it and whose lives are in jeopardy and danger."
I am simply looking for immigration based on my skills and experience. I entered this country on a visa and I want to stay here legally, like other immigrants who come from Europe or other countries. I am just looking for a legal pathway.

I don't want to ruin my entire life. I have roots back there, and I also don't want to limit myself from going back and visiting my relatives, as Louise Glück said in "Midsummer":
and for those who understood such things, the stars were sending messages:
You will leave the village where you were born
and in another country you'll become very rich, very powerful,
but always you will mourn something you left behind, even though you can't say what it was,
and eventually you will return to seek it.
The Nobel Prize in Literature for 2020 was awarded to Louise Glück.

And I certainly believe it is true, always you will mourn something you left behind, even though
you can't say what it was,
and eventually you will return to seek it.
In the end, I thanked her for her advice and left the group, walking back to the hotel. During my time in Vancouver, I thought a lot. I remember one morning when I woke up, there was a bunch of my hair on my pillow due to the stress and psychological pressure.

In the end, I made up my mind. I didn't apply for an extension of my visa or take any other action. I decided to leave on the exact departure date.
The evening before my flight, I was walking on Robson Street in downtown Vancouver when suddenly I saw my Iraqi friend, who hadn't left and had applied for asylum I walked with him, and when I told him I was leaving the next day, he started advising me not to. He took me by SkyTrain to downtown New Westminster, and we walked to the Quayside, where we took a few pictures together. He said, "Look at this beautiful place."

Considering the reasonable price of houses at that time, he urged me to stay and suggested that I apply for asylum. However, I refused and said, "Please stop. I have made up my mind and have to go."
But I will come back and apply for skilled immigration. We went back to downtown by SkyTrain, said goodbye, and hoped to see each other again here!

The next day, I checked out of the hotel early in the morning and walked to the waterfront to catch the bus to the airport.
As the bus moved through downtown and drew nearer to the airport, I found myself sinking deeper into thought, pondering what would happen if I couldn't return, making this the most challenging aspect of my journey.
When I arrived at the airport, I walked to the Cathay Pacific counter to check in. The lady at the counter, after inspecting my ticket, kindly informed me, "I'm afraid I have to change your flight; you can't proceed with this one. "Ah, the story of my life."

I asked, "What's wrong?" She replied, It's your passport, an Iranian passport. You can't stay in Hong Kong airport for a layover longer than a few hours, and unfortunately, the agent who booked the ticket wasn't aware of that.
She told me, "I will change your flight to the next one. You can drop off your luggage now. If you want to go back to the city and come back to the airport, you can." The next flight was at 2 am the following day.

I had already checked out of the hotel room, and it cost me again to go back into the city. I preferred to stay in the airport; it had been a long day, and the best way to pass the time was by reading a book.
During my visit to UBC University, I purchased a book from the university bookstore: "Dark Ages America: The Final Phase Of Empire" by Morris Berman.

I opened the book and started to read nonstop. It was an engaging book with a different perspective. "I especially liked Chapter 5, which was about the Axis of Resentment: Iran, Iraq, and Israel."I only allowed myself two breaks: one for lunch at McDonald's and one for dinner at Burger King.

Reading the book was the best idea to clear my mind and pass the time quickly, even on my way to Canada, In Hong Kong airport, I remember walking through the corridor to get to the gate for my next flight to Vancouver when two men stopped me and started questioning, "Where are you heading? Why?"

Are you carrying any luggage? How many pieces? And many questions about my trip like that, because that flight goes from Hong Kong to Vancouver after a short stop before heading to New York.And I was the only Iranian on that flight. Maybe that's why they wanted to make sure that everything was fine.
Anyway, that night I continued reading that book after midnight. During that time, I observed how many times the airport filled up and emptied out, witnessed happy people in arrivals and sad people in departures, and experienced greetings and goodbyes.

Slowly, I passed through security and walked toward the gate around my boarding time. I was sitting right in front of the gate, waiting for boarding to begin.

A gentleman came to check the tickets and boarding passes. When he got to mine, he smiled and asked me in Farsi, "Where are you going, Mr. Mohammad? Why are you leaving?"

Normally, people come here and stay! I replied, "Please, not again! I've made up my mind. I am going to leave, and I will come back when I have to, with my family."

On the board, the airplane was a Boeing 777 with lots of empty seats. A young lady was sitting right beside me. After takeoff, I told her, "If you don't mind, one of us can move to the empty seat, making it easier for us to take a rest." She moved to the empty seats beside us, and I raised the armrest to lay down. Finally, I relaxed and slept, no longer thinking about staying or leaving, until I woke up for the meal service on that long 13-hour flight.

After landing in Hong Kong, I had a short layover of around 3 hours before boarding another long-haul flight.

Right beside me, there was a guy from Saudi Arabia who wanted to talk mostly in Arabic, but I really wasn't in the mood. Unfortunately, this flight had no empty seats, and the sleep was not as relaxing as the other flight.

When I arrived in Bahrain, I arranged with my wife to leave the car in the airport parking lot since they were flying to Tehran. That way, I had the spare key and could drive home.

When I stepped out, it was the last day of August, and the weather was hot and breathtaking. The day before, I was in paradise with the most moderate temperatures.

The sun was rising flirtatiously and slowly until noon, but here the sun rises straight at 5 am and burns like hell! What a damn difference!

When I opened the car door, which had been left in the airport parking for a few weeks, a wave of intense heat hit my face. Even the steering wheel was too hot to touch, and the car tires seemed like they were about to melt onto the ground. I opened all the doors and ran the AC for a while to cool down before leaving.

The home situation was worse than the car situation. Normally, when you leave home for a few weeks, you need to run the AC for a few days to adjust the temperature.

When fine powder and dust occasionally drift into Bahrain and mix with humidity, it becomes hard to breathe, especially for people with respiratory problems like my son, who has had asthma since a young age.

I waited a few days until my family returned from Iran, and then I discussed with my wife and son the decision to apply for immigration to Canada.

Immigrating is a life-changing decision; it's one of the toughest decisions to make and carries immense responsibility. Everyone must act accordingly to their own circumstances.

It's a teamwork effort, and everyone must be involved. While it's true that we've already changed countries twice, the difference now is that I had a job lined up in each of those countries. This time, in addition to changing countries, we are facing a bigger problem: unemployment.

Unlike in Middle Eastern countries where only the father typically works and bears the responsibility, in a country like Canada, it's not feasible to sustain a living without both partners working, considering the cost of living.

Although my wife was very interested in working, she was not allowed to work in Arab countries due to their rules for foreign workers.

After the family meeting, we filled out and signed the forms, officially applying for the skilled worker immigration program in September 2007.

Yes, we embarked on a process that turned out to be the longest one in our entire lifetime. Waiting, believe me, is not easy; it's one of the most trying experiences in life.

It's like freezing your life, waiting for an update on your file or whatever documents they asked for, like proof of funds and statements showing you always have money in your account. You're afraid to invest because you might not be able to show proof of funds later on.

On the other hand, inflation doesn't wait for you or understand your situation.

Anyway, for the new school year, we switched my son from the Arabic curriculum to English, aligning our lives with the decision to immigrate to Canada.

It is hard to build your life on unknown facts; it might be happening or might not. It's about numbers, marks, and the officer who is evaluating your file.
And you've already made the biggest and hardest decision of your life, which is suspended until you know after a long time. Anyway, the only thing you can do is wait for a letter — a letter of hope or disappointment.
Every time we leave Bahrain for a vacation, I ask our watchman to keep any envelopes from Canada safe for me or slip them under our unit door.
And you wonder if it might come, and you lose time according to the deadline on the letter. This lasts for three years, and we never hear from Canadian immigration during that waiting period.

During this period, a lot of changes happened in immigration policy. Just remember, there were a million files rejected, and we are wondering if our file is included or not.
Under the new system, people were divided into those who applied before 2008 and those who applied after. Because we applied before 2008, the backlog was more than the normal waiting period, and the waiting time was extended.

Finally, by early 2010, we received a letter from immigration asking us to update our documents, such as proof of English test, proof of funds, qualifications, and various other documents, which really required time to gather together.

But we were kind of ready for that. This was the crucial stage of the process because the marking determined whether you would pass and proceed to the next step.
I was working on providing each document while I submitted the application. For exams like the IELTS, there's an expiration date. If it's over two years old, you should repeat it, and you don't know when they will ask you for that!

Another problem was confirming my educational qualifications and having them evaluated by the Canadian organization and system. I started this process in 2007, and by late 2009, I was able to finish it.
And it took a lot of time, effort, and expense. How many times I had to fly to Iran, go to the universities, and push them, only because they give the position to the least qualified person who doesn't understand or know anything about international relations and communication.

And they didn't even provide a confirmation letter. They simply took the documents you translated at a private translation office, put them in an envelope, and stamped it!
But Canadian evaluation organizations look for specific criteria that they want, and they may not understand our school system. This is especially true when you're seeking a letter for the US or Canada and need it in English.

I spent two years of my life dealing with trivial matters that should have been routine tasks: qualifications and transcripts, along with a confirmation letter in English, sealed in an envelope and sent to the organization that requested them by courier, a service for which you pay. It should have been as easy as that!
I remember when the board in Canada asked for my original documents to be submitted there, I was so worried and anxious when I sent them with prepaid DHL to make it easier for them to send them back to me.

And how many times I called them, pleading and begging over the phone, to send me back my documents safe and sound. It might not have been important to them, but those documents meant everything to me when I sent them, What if they go missing? Who would want to obtain a copy of them, and from where, and with what effort?
In the end, when I received my letter of acceptance for my qualifications, I was so happy and thought that I could receive some credits as adaptation for them, because everything seemed ready to go!
When I submitted all documents to the immigration officer, I was considering certain points for that letter.

However, in late 2010, we returned from vacation and my wife opened that special email address which we used for correspondence with immigration after submitting all documents.
It was shocking news! The application was rejected because it mentioned that we didn't have the pass marks. The pass mark at the time was 67, and mine was 65, leaving us 2 marks short!

All the plans and efforts were gone, just like that. Believe me, it wasn't easy after over 3 years of waiting; it wasn't pleasant at all.
When my son heard the news about the rejection, he innocently told me, "That means we are not going to Canada," tears dripping from his eyes. It was a breathtaking moment for all of us.
I really didn't know what I should do. My mind wasn't working at the time, and the only thing that came to my mind was talking to myself, saying, "I've already been there, and I didn't stay. I destroyed everything and hoped to make it right, but look at me now!"

I didn't have an immigration lawyer to ask what the next steps are or what I should do. My brain doesn't stop thinking, and I couldn't sleep. I've reviewed everything hundreds of times, every specific part of the ranking system.
I found out that the only part where I could make some adjustments was the language section. I could retake the IELTS exam to improve my score. This is it, the only thing I have and am able to do.
I don't have Canadian work experience, haven't studied in Canada, don't have any relatives in Canada, and don't have a job offer...

So the only thing left for me there is the language. I started to write a letter, and I opened it with a quote from Archimedes (287-212 BC): "*Give me a place to stand, and I will move the earth.*"
And I explained the honest mistake I made in calculating the marks and my expectation to receive the required mark from the board's letter, which shows I am ready to start my work in Canada, in the adaptation section. I offered, if possible, to be given another chance to achieve the pass marks.
I submitted that letter by email, which I called "**the letter of hope.**"

On the other hand, I didn't make any investment or economic planning with my money. I froze my money in bank accounts in Bahrain, just hoping that we would go to Canada and we would need it anytime they asked for proof of funds. After that, it would be for spending in Canada to start our new life there.

So, we came up with a new plan and decided to buy an apartment in Iran, at least to keep up with inflation and be prepared to return when my son started his first year of high school. He needed to be there to learn about the university entrance exam, become familiar with the school and the system, as he had never attended school in Iran before.

So, I waited for three weeks to see if I would receive any email from Canadian immigration. When I didn't receive any response, I bought a ticket to go to Iran. I withdrew my money and exchanged it for American dollars because in Iran, nobody is looking for Bahraini dinars, and the market mostly prefers American currency. The day before my trip to Iran, I opened my email and found a reply from the immigration officer responsible for my file and application.

He said, "I've decided to give you another chance. You need to show an IELTS score with a significant difference that could change your pass mark. Then, I might reopen your file and continue your process." He gave me a short period of time to submit my IELTS result.

I headed to the British Council and registered for three IELTS exams one after another. The staff there were surprised why I was taking three IELTS exams with no time gap between them. And of course, the exam fees were expensive, 80 dinars each, equivalent to $214 US dollars for every exam.

So now I am torn between two projects: one is the IELTS, the results of which could be unknown but effective on our future, and the other is a real one buying a property in Iran that I have to take action on. Now, I've learned my lesson to rely on real facts rather than an unknown dream.

So things got complicated as always; why should they be easy? I got stuck with some problems while trying to buy property in Iran, and I ended up flying there three times during my deadline for submitting the IELTS results.

Every time I traveled to Iran and returned to Bahrain, I attended an IELTS exam, a period filled with stress.
I remember during one of the exams, the Listening part, which was held in a school, the air conditioning was so noisy. I asked the examiner to turn off the AC because in my last experience with another exam, it was hard to hear the voice and answer the questions.

She didn't agree and said the weather is too hot, and no one is interested in turning the AC off. I said it's just half an hour and we could tolerate that, but she insisted no!
At that time, I stood up and looked at the students, most of whom were young Indians. The cost of the exam and the results were important to them. I explained the effect of this damn AC noise on my previous exam and how it could affect their exam results.
They all agreed to turning off the AC for the listening part, but it caused me some stress and anger. Anyway, that was my situation!
In the end, I put the exam results in an envelope and sent them to the immigration officer with a nice cover letter.

After a few weeks of waiting, I received an email from the immigration officer, but I was very nervous to open and click on it. Finally, I did what I had to do and clicked to open the email. To my surprise, I got accepted and achieved the pass mark , and They asked for the next document, which was a police certificate from each country where I spent more than six months' time. It was at the end of 2010, and they gave me 120 days to submit those police certificates.
In the very first week, I obtained our Bahraini police certificate, which was easy with a very reasonable price and time frame. However, dealing with Jordan and Iran was difficult.
We went to the Jordanian embassy in Manama, and they said no, we can't give you the police certificate. I was familiar with Jordanian morals and culture during the three years I spent there.

I asked for a time and appointment to visit the ambassador or one of the officials for that purpose, and finally, I got the appointment. I bought some Iranian pistachios and sweets, and we went to visit at our appointed time. I gave the gift to the reception and waited to get into the official's room to talk.

Finally, I entered a room and met with a lady who was kind and understanding. I talked about my problem and the issues I encountered with obtaining a police certificate from the Jordanian embassy and at the end, I reminded her that yesterday your country needed me, as I run a department at Jordan University. However, today, when I just need a piece of paper, you guys hesitate to give it to me.

Anyway, a few days later, I received a call from the Jordanian embassy informing me that the certificates are ready for pickup.
But the last one was the Iranian police certificate, which was the most annoying and difficult to obtain from them! They charged us 70 Bahraini dinars for certificates and tried to waste our time until the deadline was over.

And then by 2011, the Arab Spring had begun and reached Bahrain. Still, I hadn't received the Iranian police certificates. Every day, we followed up with them, but received no response.
Finally, we submitted the police certificates from the other two countries to immigration. In the accompanying cover letter, I explained the situation, including the Arab Spring and its consequences on the police certificate process.
On the other hand, conditions in Bahrain worsened in mid-February 2011, and the crisis escalated every day. Unfortunately, one of the central issues was at the hospital where I worked, namely Salmaniya Hospital.

At work, I witnessed numerous demonstrations within the hospital premises. One evening, we left home to buy bread from a bakery near the hospital. Suddenly, we were confronted with a strange scene. The rebels were at the hospital gates with a welding machine, welding the iron gates and , preventing people from entering or exiting the hospital.
I got a bad feeling about that, and when I saw that scene, I decided not to go to work. The next day, I stayed at home, and it lasted for two weeks. The government even shut down all the schools, and later on, they imposed a curfew for a few days.
I remember at that time, one evening we went shopping for groceries, and on our way back, I took a wrong turn onto one of the highways, leading us to the starting point of the curfew zone.

Out of habit, I turned onto a street in the Sanabis area, which was one of the most problematic areas in Manama.
The weather was getting darker as we reached the checkpoint. I didn't turn back and continued toward the checkpoint for safety reasons. Both my wife and my son were scared, and it was a stressful situation.

Finally, I stopped the car and lowered the driver side shield. There were 15 minutes left until the start of the curfew. A tall ranger, wearing a mask, from the Saudi Arabian armed forces, came to support the Bahraini government, Using Arabic words, he asked me where we were heading and why. Then, he inquired about my nationality, where I worked, and what my job was. He also requested my ID card, which had expired, but due to the situation, I couldn't renew it.
With all these factors—being Iranian, working at Salmaniya Hospital (a source of problems), having an expired ID card, and being in the Sanabis area at that checkpoint—it's understandable that the Saudi ranger had every reason not to believe me in that situation.

He took a quick look inside the car and, upon realizing that we were a family returning from shopping, he opened the gate. With a respectful tone, he said, "Welcome, doctor!"
I drove through, entered, and continued along the main street in that area, which eventually connected to the boulevard leading to our area.

The street lights were off, and various sizes of stones and bricks were scattered on the street, along with burning tires. I used the high beams to see better.
Those 15 minutes were the longest ever, as we had heard on the news that a few people who entered the curfew zone right at the start of curfew had been shot.
That was scary; we could have been hurt by both sides of the conflict, the rebels and the militias. Bullets don't distinguish between individuals in the midst of chaos.
I can hear my heart beating loudly as I grip the wheel, my eyes fixed on the road ahead. I feel regret about taking this troublesome road and making a mistake.

When we finally got out of that zone at the next checkpoint, it was a big relief. That night, I couldn't sleep and kept reviewing every second of that scene and the situation, questioning what if this had occurred or that had occurred.
Why are we here in the middle of the problems in another country, while all foreigners, especially Europeans and British, have left Bahrain under these conditions?
The smell of tear gas and mustard gas filled the atmosphere of Manama. From January to March, it's the only time of the year you can go for a walk outside at night. However, due to the smell and the effects of tear gas, especially with my son's asthma condition, it's impossible to go out.

Now, here in Bahrain, I can see what happened in Iran in 1979 and even in the years before that. The missing puzzle piece is that, because of my age, I can see and compare these two countries.
The reform was initiated in Bahrain, and you can see its effects everywhere. However, radical groups always seek change at any cost, even if it means destroying the entire country and economy, as they only prioritize their own interests and seek power.
I don't want to delve into politics and justice here, but I always prefer reform over rebellion and revolution.
To enhance your house, you don't destroy it; instead, you just need to think about what improvements you can make to increase its quality.

Anyhow, as always, the rumours start, and the thoughts about supporting the Shia radicals by the Iranian government were disturbing, fuelled by news suggesting that Iran's foreign policy and its aim to export Islamic revolution to the region and the rest of the world could be true.
Imagine we are leaving this Islamic republic, but it is not leaving us. Wherever you go, the same burden is attached to our lives. What can we really do? The money that is supposed to improve our quality of life goes elsewhere, causing problems.
It's as if the money and assets of this country are cursed, used only for theft and evil purposes.
Amidst this crisis, we are still seeking those police certificates from the Iranian embassy.

One day, while I was at work, my wife went to the embassy to follow up and asked the individual who served as the secretary and security officer of the embassy.

I'm not mentioning his name here. He was there with his entire family, all of them crying and saddened because the Bahraini government gave them 48 hours to leave the country.
It was his last days of work at the embassy. When my wife asked and insisted, he said it might come, and he issued the police certificates. He handed them from the room window to another person, pretending they had just arrived from Iran when he had actually entered from the main entrance door of the embassy building.

Yes, we received the Iranian police certificates during the last minutes of his work in Bahrain, causing a few months' delay in our immigration process. Finally, we submitted them to immigration and proceeded to the next step, which involved background and security checks. Due to changes in a few countries, it took a long time to complete this process.
For a few months, going to work wasn't pleasant because the army was stationed at the hospital gates. To enter the gate, they checked your ID and questioned you, with different guards on different shifts every day.
On the other hand, I still have the expired residency card that they ask for all the time, and I have to explain again and again that because of the situation, I haven't renewed it yet!

I remember one day, a young soldier who seemed to enjoy wielding his gun and power was stationed at the entrance gate, checking people and questioning them in the morning. When I entered after a physical examination and bag check, he began questioning me.
"Do you have any problem with Sunni people? Do you have a problem with Sheikh Khalifa?" These are silly questions. When someone has a gun, you should be very careful when answering their questions!
But eventually, the army left the hospital, and only police officers continued security at the main hospital building entrance. They began installing security cameras everywhere in hospitals.

They have the right to do that because rumours said that the rebels have a plan in Bahrain similar to the one Hezbollah had in Lebanon, aiming to occupy hospitals, airports, and other strategic locations. However, they forgot that Bahrain is different, and their plans didn't succeed.
All the direct flights from Iran to Bahrain was stopped and it was more difficult and cost more for us to going to Iran now , we have to go through the Emirates or Qatar.

A one-and-a-half-hour flight turned into a journey of several hours with layovers and increased costs! Being Iranian, every day brings us more surprises from our mother country. We always seem to pay more and gain less than other nations in the world!
Finally, by the end of 2012, we received an email from immigration asking for some updated documents like proof of funds and police certificates from the last country we had spent time in, which was Bahrain. We gathered them and submitted them.
Because they always ask for the original documents, you have to send them by courier, and I preferred DHL, which works better than any others in Middle Eastern countries.
After a few weeks, in the early days of 2013, we received another email for a medical examination, which is the last stage of the process. According to immigration, we have to undergo all medical examinations at the American hospital in Manama under the trusted doctor there.

So we underwent all tests, and everything was fine except for me! During the last examination, my blood pressure was too high, and it hasn't returned to normal. To be honest, I wasn't surprised, given the stressful life, especially the recent situation. Therefore, the doctor referred me to another specialist.
We have to visit the cardiologist. Luckily, his office was in a private hospital close to our home. We booked an appointment to visit him. The next day, we returned for the appointment. The good thing about private sector services is that"No waiting list or any other kind of delay."
He was an amazing doctor with a great personality. He conducted every possible test to confirm that I had hypertension and needed treatment. I was ignorant and believed that recent life excitement had caused my blood pressure to increase.

It will get better soon, but it hasn't, especially during the last two weeks. I tried everything, like watermelon, cranberry... everything that might bring down the blood pressure, as I was shaking inside, but my blood pressure was still high.

I tried my best to improve my medical exam results before the referral to the cardiologist, but the stubborn number didn't change, and it even got worse after a few attempts. The doctor said I had to visit a specialist, which is why I'm here now.
Even the cardiologist connected a machine to my arm that takes my blood pressure every half hour for 24 hours. When he printed the results, it showed that I had high blood pressure even during deep sleep, so he prescribed medicine for me.

And he assured immigration that my heart would be okay for the next 5 years! So, in the end, our medical examination was completed, and the hospital submitted it to immigration.
A month later, we received an email from immigration asking us to submit our passports to the Canadian embassy in London and pay the fees by Visa card for the issuance of the permanent visa and landing papers.

They always ask for a bank draft or cheque, but this time the payment has to be made by Visa card. And in Arab countries at that time, they were not issuing visa cards to foreign nationals. When were things ever easier for us? They asked for something that I don't have!
On the other hand, I don't want to ask any friends to use their Visa card because I don't want anyone to know about my decision to go.So we went to the Bahrain National Bank and asked what we could do about it. Luckily, there was an informed and updated guy whom I knew from before due to my banking experience with that branch.
He said there is a new type of visa card that was recently released, called the refill visa card, which could help you.
That was a relief. I immediately applied for that card, which takes two weeks to issue, and I went to the main branch of the Bahrain National Bank in Manama to get it.

So finally, we did that and paid for the permanent visa fees. We printed the receipt and enclosed it in the same envelope with our passports, then submitted it via DHL to the Canadian embassy in London.

We were happy and hoped to get our passports back with the visa and landing papers within 4 weeks, but the happiness didn't last long due to the news. We were informed that for the first time in Canadian foreign affairs history, their staff were being stopped from working due to a strike.

Wow! We definitely needed to hear that news. I followed up with an email to see if our status was affected by the strikes, and they replied, "Yes, it's been affected."
We are in the middle of preparing to sell the car, packing up, getting rid of stuff, ending the rental agreement, and dealing with all the other related tasks. We've also got tickets to fly back to Iran for the summer vacation and plan to go to Vancouver before school starts.

We reserved tickets for Vancouver, and now we're stuck because of the strikes. So we have to postpone everything again, pay rent for an extended period, and reschedule everything, but we have no idea when.
It took a long time, and we didn't even have our passports to go for summer vacations. In late July, around noon, while I was at work, my cell phone started ringing. It was a stranger's number. I answered the phone, and a DHL guy with a nice Indian accent asked for my name and said he had a package for me from the Canadian embassy.
He said, "I am on my way to drop off your package at your home address." I quickly called my wife, and she went to the nearest ATM machine close to home to withdraw some cash for tips to give to the DHL guy. She tipped him 20 dinars.

Finally, we got it—the project that had been in my mind since early youth. We spent the last decade of our lives working towards it, and we have been waiting for the last 6 years with all the stress and anxiety. Now, it's here! We got permanent residency in Canada!

We went out that night to a good French restaurant to celebrate our achievements—a beautiful night filled with fun, laughter, excitement, and even more enthusiasm for the next season of our adventure together.
Cheering for another horizon of hope! Deep down, I know it will be difficult and more challenging, but it gives us a reason to be grateful, happy, and celebrate something we have accomplished.
We changed our round-trip ticket to a one-way ticket and upgraded to a first-class ticket to create good memories as we leave Bahrain after 7.5 years.
Everything was arranged, and I got my vacation leave. I just told my friend that we were leaving, and he said, "I will take you to the airport." We had one last coffee together, had such a great time, and had a brief goodbye party at airport.

We arrived late, after midnight, in Tehran and drove to Qazvin for three hours. After a few hours, we returned to Tehran, to the Lufthansa office in north Tehran, to finalize our ticket reservations and payments.
This was the time when the value of the Iranian Rial started to decline, and the price of the dollar was unstable. We paid some in dollars and some in rials. We purchased one-way tickets, which was a first for me.
It seems like I understand that if I have round-trip tickets, I might not stay in Canada because deep down, I know what life is like there when you are unemployed, facing high living costs, and have limited financial resources.

You have made a commitment that you can support yourself for one year, and everyone knows it's not easy to get the first job in Canada, especially the first full-time permanent job, even with minimum wages. This is particularly challenging because you need full-time employment for both spouses to afford a basic lifestyle in big cities.
Part of your mind is happy that you're embarking on a new experience, but the other part is fearful of unemployment and surviving the start of a new life.
Especially challenging in immigration are skilled workers, as they often struggle to find employment in their own field after immigrating.

With all these thoughts in mind, we endeavoured to enjoy our final moments together in Iran, striving to create the most positive atmosphere and fulfillment before facing the storm that awaits us after this calm.

Sometimes you wish to achieve something or reach a certain place, but when the time comes, you wish you hadn't made that wish.
Those days flew by so quickly. That was the last summer we were all able to be in Iran together. Since then, we haven't had a chance to gather in Iran again, as it's been difficult to make arrangements.

My son couldn't go due to mandatory military service. If he set foot in Iran, he would be unable to leave and would have to fulfill his military service obligation. Even when they issued a new Iranian passport for him, they mentioned this requirement on the passport.Thanks to Reza Shah for instituting this foolish law of compulsory military service in Iran.
Our clinic closed during the period between the end of the year and the new year, which resulted in the loss of several of my vacation days. Due to my wife's work in retail, which experiences peak sales season at the end and beginning of the new year, she couldn't take vacation days during that time.

So officially, it's not possible to repeat those days.
We were close to packing up and getting ready to leave. Each one of us has a limit of carrying two luggage, but we decided to take just one instead because we believe it will be much easier to move between cities over there.

By the evening of September 9th, we left. The goodbye this time was harder for everyone because we were going far away, and we don't know when we might see each other again.
In the early morning on September 10th, we flew to Frankfurt, and after a short layover, we caught the second flight to Vancouver.

4

Canada

Finally, we landed in Vancouver by the afternoon of September 10th! It felt like time traveling, saving time!
This time, we have to go through immigration because we are landed immigrants, and we have some paperwork to complete before entering the country.
So, after waiting in line for a few hours and passing through the immigration office, we answered the questions that the officer asked us.
At the entrance, before the exit door, there was another counter for providing information to new immigrants. When we got there,We had smiles on our faces as the guy gave us information and brochures, saying, "Hopefully, you can keep these smiles forever."
Oops! What is he talking about? We didn't take it seriously because he continued, saying that many people could not maintain those smiles after they started living here.
So we got out of the airport and took a taxi to the hotel downtown that I had booked for a week. On our way to the hotel, the taxi driver started chatting, and we found out that he was an educated person back home, but here he is a cab driver.

Finally, we reached the hotel reception and checked in. It feels so good knowing that you've already paid for everything in advance, and now you don't have to think about payment anymore.
It was a tough time after the Great Recession, which refers to the economic downturn from 2007 to 2009 following the bursting of the U.S. housing bubble and the global financial crisis.

Even in 2013, when you walked on the street, you could see shops that had shut down and businesses that had left, with many homeless people, especially in downtown areas. On our first evening, we went to eat dinner and bought groceries and some food.
My son, who had never seen so many homeless people before, was scared and didn't want to go out anymore after sunset.
So the next day, we began our day with formal official tasks, such as going to Service Canada to obtain SIN numbers and going to the bank to open accounts and deposit our money.
We spent the following days searching for a place to rent that would be close to the school. Since school had already started and we had limited time staying at the hotel, we needed to find a place that was both livable and affordable.

Due to my previous trip to Vancouver, I had a paper map of Greater Vancouver, and I did my homework beforehand, thanks to the internet, which has grown significantly over the last few years.
I wrote a brief summary for each area on the map for a quick look, and for the first three days staying at the hotel, I stayed awake late searching for a rental apartment. They were very expensive even at that time.
Finally, I found a place in New Westminster, which was close to the Burnaby area and had easy access to public transportation, particularly the SkyTrain, which was just a few blocks away. The school was also close enough to walk to and quite accessible.
We called a taxi to get there, and because the driver chose the Trans Canada Hwy, we felt like we were leaving the town and started thinking about how difficult the everyday commute would be in this city in the future.
Living in Bahrain, one of the smallest countries in the world, made us lose the sense of what it's like to live in big cities, and that perception was removed from our minds.

Sometimes it was difficult to estimate the required travel time between different areas of the town where we had appointments.
I prefer to rent from large rental cooperation companies instead of individuals. It was the right choice for us, and in their ads, they offered one month of free rent, which was perfect for us.
At that time, you could see these kinds of offers due to the aftermath of the economic crisis. But now, some individuals demand the entire year's rental fee from newcomers who don't have a job or credit.

We had the necessary documentation that they needed to sign the contract, including a void cheque and bank statements.

So the building manager didn't mention anything about the one month of free rent, but I reminded her. At first, she said no, saying she didn't know about it, but I insisted that I saw it on your website. I even showed her a screenshot of the advertisement.

So, she checked the website and said we could save it for the last month, but I said I prefer to have it in the first month because I need it now. We paid the deposit, and in the end, we got the key. That was a relief because now we have an address, and we can apply for school.
Right after that, we went to the school and talked about the registration and the procedure. I'll never forget that at the reception, the receptionist, upon finding out that we were coming from the Middle East, said, 'Now you are here, out of the war zone!'
I remember, I replied, 'Please, ma'am, study some geography and politics. Let's not talk about this stuff.'
On our way back, we found out that the sky train is a few blocks away, so we walked from uptown New West to downtown. While we were walking down the street, a guy sitting on his rental apartment balcony shouted, 'Go back to your fucking country!'
He knows that we are newcomers and shows some excitement! We didn't take it seriously.
We went back to the hotel in downtown. Then, in the evening, we went to London Drugs in downtown and bought some cooking supplies.

We also purchased a small smart TV from Best Buy.Because we had to move to the apartment by taxi, it was easier to take the necessary stuff without a car.

Finally, after about two days, we moved into our rental apartment. The apartment was quiet and empty, with every sound echoing in it. We didn't even have a blanket to sleep, so I googled the nearest IKEA, and my wife and I went to shop for some blankets and pillows.

Luckily, they had just renewed the apartment, and the carpet was new. We also got extra blankets that could be used as a mattress for sleeping.
Never forget that with so much shopping and our hands full, we forgot our way back to the sky train station. We arrived there by bus and were not familiar with the bus stop to return to the sky train station. We didn't have data on our mobile phones to search for directions and asked a few people, but they didn't know either.
So finally, after walking up and down the highway a few times, we finally found the way to get to the station. Even now, whenever we pass through that area, we still remember that day and laugh.

It seems like you're perceiving things mostly through your brain rather than your vision, because when your brain is full of stress and busy, you can't see anything clearly or even remember simple things.
We still had a lot of things to do. We had already applied for Hydro and Internet, but the technician wouldn't come until a week later. In the meantime, we had to use the public library's wifi.
One of those very first days when we went to the library to use our laptop and the internet, my wife forgot her purse there. It wasn't just a purse; it contained everything important: our landing papers, passport, jewelry, cash, credit cards, and bank cards.

When we got home, we realized that the purse wasn't there. She had forgotten to take it from the library chair where she left it.That was a devastating mistake, with no money to even pay the rent and without passports or landing papers, which made everything more difficult.

We rushed back to the library, but it was closed and no one was there. I saw that they had placed the purse close to the main door, where you could somehow see it.
It was a little relief, but we weren't worried about the purse; we were worried about the things inside it. When we got home, we called the bank and canceled the cards to minimize any potential damage.

The next early morning, before the library opened, we were there. When they opened the door, we went to the reception and asked for the missing purse. We provided all the information about the items inside it, showed some ID cards, and retrieved the purse.
Everything was there, and nothing was missing. That was quite a relief, and it was hard to believe that we had the purse back untouched.
We had never experienced anything like that before, forgetting or missing anything, but stress and busy minds caused this strange thing to happen.

When the internet was installed at home, it felt much better. Nowadays, without internet, you feel disconnected from the world. I wonder if it's possible to live without internet.
By the third week after the settlement, we started applying for jobs and dropping off our CVs. By the fourth week, I had my first appointment with the general manager of one of the clinics that has few different branches in the Lower Mainland.
During the interview, I had all the necessary information and documents with me. Additionally, I had obtained the Board letter after spending a couple of years to obtain it, which made me fully prepared to secure a job, as they confirmed I was ready to go!
In the interview, the first question he asked me wasn't professional. He inquired why I came to Canada. If you were in my position, how would you respond to someone asking this question?
That day, I wore a full suit, necktie, and polished shoes, and I also wore cologne, as American interview advisors suggest, to present the best appearance of oneself.
I was quite flexible regarding any potential changes in position; I simply didn't want to remain jobless and waste my energy and experience in fields unrelated to my own profession.

I had everything necessary for this profession: a bunch of certifications from reputable institutions in Germany, Sweden, and Finland for practical training, and years of experience, and the Board letter in our field as well as legal immigrant status. What else do you need from me?

I left that office empty-handed, experiencing my first rejection and feeling disheartened about my immigration to Canada, as the guy asked me, "Why are you coming here?" I wanted to ask him, "Why are you here too?"

Because everyone here is an immigrant, either they came by themselves like me, or their parents or previous generations, like grandparents. What kind of question is that to ask in an interview?

On my way back on the sky train, with my mind still preoccupied with that question, a young black girl, who seemed dissatisfied with the capitalist system, approached me and loudly asked, "Do you enjoy wearing nice suits like the white guys?"

And she continued talking like that. I was surprised by what was really going on here.

The other day, while walking with my wife down the road in New Westminster, a middle-aged black man saw us smiling, talking, and walking. He initiated a quick chat and asked, "Where are you from?" We replied, "Persian, from Iran."

He said, "I know that from the Bible. You are new here, but soon you will not laugh like that anymore!" His words made me ponder and question whether we made a good decision by coming here.

I didn't give up and continued dropping off my CV. I got a second interview at another clinic and facility while I was still dropping off my CV.

When we sat down to talk, the guy was quite impressed by my CV but had a strange tendency to make things seem like they were not going anywhere. He brought up a story about his Persian patient.

He mentioned that the patient wanted to stay in Canada as a refugee. He asked him to prolong his visit and make his leg in a longer time to give him more time and similar considerations.

I told him I wasn't sure if that story was relevant to my job search here because I am a legal immigrant and I am here under the skilled worker class with permanent residency status.

In the end, when he realized I wasn't happy with that conversation, he said, "I am an immigrant too!" I replied, "Good to hear. Who isn't an immigrant in Canada except the indigenous people? Why should we have had this conversation in the first place?"

I was there for a few hours, and my poor wife was waiting outside, hoping that I would get a job soon! I continued to drop off my CV at clinics throughout the city, but there were no opportunities.
My wife got disappointed, and she told me that if they are not giving me a chance, how about her? Psychologically, it doesn't feel good to her.
I started sending out CVs, making phone calls, and emailing contacts across the country. I applied and sent out my CV, 120 times, and kept following up, but received no response.

We both tried, but as the days passed, the money in our bank accounts dwindled rapidly, like snow melting in front of the sun. Starting a new life is always costly, and expenses were high.
The cost of living never stops until you get settled and find your place in the new world with a proper job and position. Bills don't care about your situation; they keep coming day after day.
There was a booklet titled "Welcome to Canada." On page 95, there was a picture and story of a gentleman named Michel Cubric, who arrived in Canada from Brazil in 1995, washing dishes in a restaurant kitchen.

And said; *I did not have any connections, so like a lot of newcomers I took on a number of odd jobs in order to provide for my family. I cleaned the kitchen at a local restaurant, sold electronics at a small store and even tried delivering the morning paper.*
It was a big change for Cubric, who was a senior flight attendant for a Brazilian airline and travelled all over the world.
I never forget that story. Many people don't pay attention to it when I talk with them. So, one day, I saw an advertisement from a company, and I told my wife, "Let's go to their office in Vancouver and apply for that job." It was one of those survival jobs, involving hard work with minimum payment.

We had to start from scratch; they weren't going to offer us a professional job as our first job in Canada. This is a common practice, and I can feel it.

It's good for business! It's a good way to lower the cost of skilled workers! He lowers his expectations, and if by any chance he gets an opportunity, he will accept it with the minimum professional wage.

It's good for the employer and for you as an employee because you don't want to go back to those survival jobs, and you prefer to accept the job with that salary.

On the other hand, they undermine your self-confidence and somehow imply that you don't know anything.

Those days were long and challenging to overcome. Each of us managed to secure two jobs: one full-time job where my wife and I worked together, and one part-time job on Saturdays where we worked in different jobs and places.

My son went to school during the day, and when he came home in the afternoon, we had to leave for work, leaving him home alone.

I remember once when we were cleaning his room, we found a knife under his blanket. We realized this because we often came home after midnight, and he was afraid to be alone. Although he was 13, it was the first time in his life that he had to be alone.

But what can we do? We need to put bread on the table and have a roof over our heads!

I'll never forget when that movie, "12 YEARS A SLAVE," came out. While watching it, I cried throughout, especially during the scene when Chiwetel Ejiofor shouted, *"I was a free man! I am not a slave!"*

Those dark days! Once, I was standing on one of those high-rise buildings, on one of the top floors, in front of the window, and watching the city. The entire city was in front of me, and I questioned God: "In this big city, there is no place for us. Why?"

Immigration breaks you down inside; you feel vulnerable and devastated. It's as if you lose your identity.

We continued working, alongside obtaining the driver's license and other important documents. However, everything was still done in the worst possible manner.

Even the immigration law changed again after we landed. According to the new law, you need to stay in the country for 4 years instead of 3 years to be eligible to apply for citizenship.

The funny part was when we applied after 4 years, they changed it back to 3 years! This change caused my son, who had started wrestling and had earned the third place in Canada in Greek style, to be unable to attend American tournaments and join the national team.

During those times, we set a deadline for our stay in the country. We decided to stay until the end of the summer of 2014. If I found a job in my profession, we would stay; if not, we would leave Canada forever.

I hate this kind of talk that I sometimes hear from some parents, saying, "We came here for the future of our children!"

What future are you talking about? As a vulnerable parent earning minimum wage, what kind of future can you afford to provide for your children? When you can barely put bread on the table and pay the rent, what exactly are you talking about here?

For this matter, we came up with a deadline. Generally, we base our decision on the IF-THEN principle: if this happens, then I do this or that. In this case, if I get into my profession, then we will stay.

After about 8 months had passed, I began applying and dropping off CVs again, maintaining the same level of activity. However, this time it was much easier because we had obtained the driver's license and a car.

Every morning, my wife and I drove to different offices across the Lower Mainland to drop off our CVs. By evening, we had to go to work together. Finally, I got an interview and kept following up, leading to a second interview at the same place. In the end, I got the job!

That day was fateful! Those moments are unforgettable. On my way back home, I took a wrong turn and it took longer to get home. The best part was when I shared the news with my wife; she was ecstatic, jumping up and down and screaming!

That was a good vibe since we moved here. When my son arrived home from school and we shared the news with him, he got happy too, and he said, "Finally, we are going to stay!"
Because every day when he got back from school, he asked, "When will we leave?" It seems like my son is living in limbo, which isn't good for a young boy his age who wants to make friends. He should have a place to live that he can call home.

It was difficult for him to change countries again and lose his friends and connections at this age.
Even a few times, we considered changing our place or had the chance to buy an apartment in different areas of the city, but he insisted that he didn't want to move to another area and until the years after he graduated from high school, we didn't move from that area.
So, for the last week, we went to work together, and I quit that job at the end of the week and started the new job at the beginning of the next week.

Even my wife and I quit our Saturday jobs to try to spend the weekend together, and every evening I had more time to spend with my son.
Still, sometimes I thought about those 8 months when we had to leave him alone, which caused some gaps between us.

In The Alchemist (P-24), Paulo Coelho discusses the concept of the Personal Legend: *But what exactly is the Personal Legend?*
It's what you have always wanted to accomplish. Everyone when they are young, knows what their Personal Legend is.
At that point in their lives, everything is clear and everything is possible. They are not afraid to dream, and to yearn for everything they would like to see happen to them in their lives. But, as time passes, a mysterious force begins to convince them that it will be impossible for them to realize their Personal Legend.
But what the "mysterious force "is?
It's a force that appears to be negative, but actually shows you how to realize your Personal Legend. It prepares your spirit and your will, because there is one great truth on this planet:

whoever you are, or whatever it is that you do, when you really want something, it's because that desire originated in the soul of the universe.
It's your mission on earth.

Even when all you want to do is travel? Or marry the daughter of a textile merchant?
Or even search for treasure. The Soul of the World is nourished by people's happiness. And also by unhappiness, envy, and jealousy. To realize one's Personal Legend is a person's only real obligation. All things are one.
And , when you want something, all the universe conspires in helping you to achieve it.

Wow! I never get tired of these sentences; I could keep reading them all the time!
Personal Legend, mysterious force!

Since my youth, I've known my Personal Legend: to come to Canada. However, due to various mysterious events, I had nothing. Despite battling these mysterious forces, we persevered. Everything that happened along our journey helped us understand ourselves and Canada better.

When we attempted to resign from our Saturday jobs, they said it was a mistake, but we are clear about our intentions; we want to spend more quality time together as a family.
It might be meaningless for some people, but for us, it has significance. When we reflect on those days, I thought we would never regain a sense of normalcy in our lives, and our lifestyle seemed ruined and we will never be able to go for evening walks together or spend weekends together again.
This kind of experience is priceless.
A year and a half later, my wife found a job close to home, and she can walk there. Slowly, everything returned to normal. Even though we flew back to Iran for a visit, we did so with caution and not together Because it costs more, and we have to take additional days off without pay.

In the first year, we spent some time counting the days needed for the citizenship application, but later, we didn't even think about it until after the fourth year, when we realized we had to apply for citizenship.

This was the last time we finally had to gather all the documents together and apply for citizenship.
We submitted our application, and after that, everything moved quickly, unlike the excruciating waiting times before immigration and its processes. The citizenship test and interview were the final steps, and they went smoothly.

After a short time, we received an email for the citizenship ceremony, which was the final correspondence with the immigration office.
The last waiting period before attaining citizenship finally came to an end on Tuesday, April 3, 2018, when we became Canadian citizens. It was a momentous day for us, filled with a strange yet profound feeling, as if our entire life flashed before our eyes in that moment.

All those moments, moments of hope and despair, joy and sadness, laughter and crying. Why couldn't you have this feeling in your homeland?I could see this emotion on all the faces of those who were at the ceremony with us, most of whom had teary eyes.

Where the Prime Minister concludes with pleasant words: *"Thank you for choosing Canada. Welcome home."*

Home is the most beautiful word and place. On that day, we surrendered our PR cards and received our citizenship certificates instead.
All the temporary residencies we had in other countries, and the time and effort spent renewing them, are over now. We are finally home.
As they say, 'home sweet home!' From the bottom of our hearts, we are proud to be part of this wonderful country and its diversity.

By the beginning of the next week after the ceremony, we applied for our passports. On Thursday, May 17, 2018, we received our passports, and by Sunday, May 20, 2018, we took our first trip to the United States, visiting Seattle.

The first time I traveled to the United States, a very serious and composed immigration officer asked me, 'What is your job?'
I replied, "I work in prosthetic field." He then asked, "If my hand is ever cut, could you make an artificial one for me?" I responded, God forbid. I hope you always stay healthy and never need my services.

In my youth, my friends called me "American Mohammad" because despite all the negative advertisements about America, I always loved America and its system, and I still do.
I hope for a day when everyone can see America; in my opinion, America, and also Canada, represent the pinnacle of human achievement.

These diverse nations, along with every religion, idea, and language, embody the slogan: Productivity = Diversity^2.
That was a great experience, and for the first time, I was able to visit America without any visa requirements. On our way, my wife and I discussed everything we had always heard about America since school, reviewing every story.

They tried to portray America as falling apart and such, but it was all emotional for us. We visited the Future of Flight and Boeing Company, which was an incredible experience.
At every step in America, we reminisced about those days back in our childhood in Iran when they talked about the enemy.

Different kinds of enemies: external, internal, international enemies! War! War! Until Victory! Down with America! What happened?

What a waste of time and energy resources! It seems the easiest solution to confront a problem is to blame it all on others!" - Paul Ham, in the book "Young Hitler: The Making of the Fuhrer

On page 247, a very important question is raised: How could Hitler have happened? The simple answer: Hitler was the bastard child of the First World War and the economic and social chaos that followed.

What happened to us was exactly the same: Pahlavi's incompetence in managing state affairs and reforms, international relations, social welfare, and religious transition led to the birth of Khomeini.

As the great Iranian poet Hafez says:

Ease is the interpretation of these two letters: Deal kindly with friends, deal gently with enemies.
If we ever applied this verse to our personal, social life, and international relations, we would have a completely different situation today.

As mentioned in the book "Funky Business" by Jonas Ridderstråle and Kjell A. Nordström,
The Christianity owes its progress to Martin Luther, who changed their slogan from "pray, pray" to "work and pray!"

We do need the same thing in the Islamic world. We need to understand the new world, the Funky Business!

We transformed oil from a business and commercial product into a political, religious, and national product, making it difficult to deal with the modern world.

Any changes in the international market and needs had an impact on the entire country's economy, management system, structure, and any revolutions.
The once business product, oil, has become a tool to establish dictatorship.

Governments use oil money to purchase weapons and oppress the nation.

Felicity Jones's speech in the beautiful movie 'On the Basis of Sex,' based on a true story, was succinct. She made an interesting point while delivering her speech in the courtroom scene:
We are not asking you to change the country, that's already happened without any courts permission.
We are asking you to protect the right of the country to change!

Unfortunately, we never have this opportunity in our system to protect the right of the country to change!

That's why we never had reform or reached this phase of our path to democracy, and every chance of change always ended up in a revolution.

If the government voluntarily starts the change, it is a reform, but if the people start to change the system and the government, then it's a revolution.

In our path to prosperity, we have tried and are still trying. When I look back to those days when we arrived with three luggages and hoped that we could make it happen through this difficult and hard way, we did it all together.

I believe the entire process of immigration is like being an immigrant going to the train station. The train represents the host country, and it appears full with everyone settled in their own seats. The train doesn't even stop at the station to wait for you to get in. You have to jump on the train; you might be able to get in or not. But if you can get in, the next challenge is to find your own spot on the train. This is a real challenge for immigrant people.

Today, we are celebrating our success in our journey. Although we may not have reached the Canadian dream, or there may be no hope of achieving that dream, or maybe there is no dream called the Canadian dream at all and it was a creation of our minds.

Despite all of this, we enjoy having dinner together on the weekend and discussing what happened during the week or sharing the decisions we've made.

The only thing that we still endure is the last scene in Animal Farm, beautifully explained by George Orwell;

The creatures outside looked from pig to man, and from man to pig , and from pig to man again: but already it was impossible to say which was which.

Couldn't believe that we lived that fairy story in the real world, right up to the last scene, which was so pathetically painful.

When we look carefully, we see that the same ones who destroyed our lives, along with their children, are living luxurious lives in Canada and America with the big money they stole from us. It seems they have achieved their dream!
And maybe they were right that war is a blessing; for them, war was a blessing in every way.

For us who have been injured in the war, the war was not a blessing; it was full of crime and betrayal.

And still, we are fighting with problems every day to live a honourable life.

Glossary

Shah King, Mohammad Reza Pahlavi was the last king of Iran ,reigning before the Islamic Revolution.

Cyrus Commonly known as Cyrus the Great, was the founder of the Achaemenid Persian Empire.

Khomeini Ruhollah Khomeini, Iranian Shiite religious leader who ruled Iran after the 1979 revolution that overthrew Mohammad Reza Shah Pahlavi.

Khamenei Ali Khamenei who has served as the second supreme leader of Iran since 1989.

Karbala Is a city in central Iraq, located about 100 km southwest of Baghdad. The city, best known as the location of the Battle of Karbala in 680 AD, or for the shrines of Hussain and Abbas.

Al - Aqsa Mosque A mosque in old city of Jerusalem, initially, Muslims faced Al-Aqsa Mosque during prayer before the qibla was changed to Kaaba in Mecca.

Amir al - Mu'minin or Commander of the Faithful is a Muslim title designating the supreme leader of an Islamic community.

Quran The central religious text of Islam, believed by Muslims to be a revelation directly from God.

Surah Al - Waqi'ah The 56th Surah (chapter) of the Quran.

Sunni The largest branch of Islam, followed by 85-90% of the world's Muslims.

Shia The second largest branch of Islam after Sunni Islam.

Imam In Shia Islam, the term Imam is used to denote specific historical figures who are considered divinely appointed leaders and spiritual successor to the prophet Muhammed.

Al - Sayyida Zainab The daughter of Imam Ali, commonly known as Sitt Zainab, in Damascus, the national capital of Syria.

Moharram The first month of the Islamic calendar which a set of religious rituals observed by Shia Muslims during the month of Moharram.

Arba'in In Shia Islam, Arba'in marks forty days after Ashura, which is the martyrdom anniversary of Imam Hussein.

Matam The term used in south Asia for the act of self-flagellation during the Sia remembrance of Moharram.

Aza Includes mourning congregations, lamentations, matam and all such action which express the emotions of grief, and anger.

Turbah - Mohr Is a small piece of soil or clay, often a clay tablet, used during Shia Islam daily prayers to symbolize earth.

Mojahedin group (organization) Is an Iranian dissident organization that was previously armed but has now transitioned primarily into a political advocacy group. The group's ideology is rooted in Islam with revolutionary marxism. Its headquarters are currently in Albania.

Hezbollah or party of God, is a Lebanese Shia Islamist. It adopted the model set out by Khomeini after the Iranian Revolution in 1979, and the party founders adopted the name Hezbollah as chosen by Khomeini. Its armed strength is assessed to be equivalent to that of a medium - sized army.

Taliban Is an Afghan militant movement with an ideology comprising elements of Pashtun nationalism and the Deobandi movement of islamic fundamentalism

We were a generation that just wanted to live a somewhat normal life , but alas, fate had a different plan for us. Our life story became the same as George Orwell's "Animal Farm," and we lived that fairy story in the real world, page by page to the very last line!

Manufactured by Amazon.ca
Bolton, ON